Early Days
in
South Park

Laura Van Deusen

Early Days
in
South Park

Parked in the Past

Laura Van Dusen

EARLY DAYS IN SOUTH PARK
Copyright © 2016 by Laura Van Dusen
All rights reserved

Front cover: Abandoned cabin of an early resident, one of many that dot the landscape of South Park. *Photo by the author.*

Back cover: Street scene at South Park City Museum in Fairplay. At far left is the Stage Coach Inn, formerly the Half-Way House stage stop in Mosquito Gulch. *Photo by the author.*

First published July 2016

Edited by Tom Locke

Published by Vandusenville Publications
P. O. Box 445
Como, Colorado 80432
ParkedInThePast@gmail.com
www.facebook.com/parkedinthepast

Printed in the United States of America
by Frederic Printing, Denver, Colorado

ISBN: 978-0-692-72310-4
Library of Congress Control Number: 2016908853

The information in this book is true and complete to the best of the author's knowledge. It is offered without guarantee on the part of the author or publisher. The author and publisher disclaim all liability in connection with the use of this book.

Dedicated to Mom and Dad

Also by Laura Van Dusen

Historic Tales from Park County: Parked in the Past

Table of Contents

Table of Contents

Acknowledgments

For his courteous and entertaining way of clarifying details of South Park history, I am especially grateful to Erik Swanson. He shared photos from his collection, including a photo album given to him years ago. It contained a few photos of his mother and many photos of Willia Hamilton Johnson, her friends, and scenes from their lives in Alma. It once belonged to Willia, the subject of chapter 16. With Erik's blessing, the album was returned (with the exception of the photos of his mother) to Willia's family after her great-grandniece was located during research for this book.

Thanks also go to Erik for sharing details of his uncle Ed Snell's life for the final story in this book. It links a historic tale of early Alma homesteaders with an account of two 1980s-era drinking-buddy construction workers, who unintentionally began the Ed Snell Memorial Run, a nonprofit fundraising organization providing emergency assistance to Park County residents.

I also thank Erik and his wife Beth Swanson, for allowing me to photograph Edith Teter's 1960s-era telephone for chapter 18. It was for sale at their store, Fairplay Antique and Art Gallery, in January 2016.

I am extremely grateful to Mark and Elizabeth Stone, for allowing use of letters written in the 1860s by one of their ancestors, Colorado Supreme Court Justice Wilbur Fisk Stone, and for providing photographs of Justice Stone.

Thanks also go to Carol Davis and Cindy Huelsman of South Park City Museum for allowing me to climb aboard the restored stagecoach displayed there. Sitting inside the stagecoach and atop the driver's seat gave me a better understanding of nineteenth-century travel. I am appreciative of South Park City's extensive collection of nineteenth-century medicines, some of which I photographed for chapter 13.

Kimberly Unger, Jeremy Allen, and Stacy Chesney of Denver Water, and Garver Brown with the Colorado Division of Water Resources were indispensable in providing facts for chapter 6, Antero Reservoir. I also thank Denver Water for use of its 1941 photo of the High Line Canal.

I thank George Cassady for sharing George Geoffrey Miller's manuscript, *The Link History, A Colorado Pioneer Family.*

My conversations with Kurt House of Old West Collectibles in San Antonio, Texas, were vital in narrowing down to two choices the type of gun awarded to Lewis Link in 1880, and I thank him for sharing his knowledge. I'm grateful to Paul Goodwin for letting me use his photos of Kurt's guns to illustrate chapter 9.

I am indebted to Ricki Ramstetter, owner of Mountain Man Gallery in Como, for letting me photograph the collection of worn-out shoes previously owned by residents of the long-deserted town of King, Colorado.

Special thanks go to Sharon Amos, for sharing stories and photographs of her great-grandaunt, Willia Hamilton Johnson.

I also thank those that donated photographs for use in this book, including Larry Coats, adjunct assistant professor of geography, University of Utah; South Park Ranger District of the Pike National Forest; Bill Eloe for use of a rare 1883 George Mellen photo of Como; Colorado Historic Newspapers Collection; Emery County (Utah) Archives; Utah Historic Newspapers Collection; Doug Stiverson; and Kathy Reeves. Photographs found in the public domain from Wikimedia Commons and from Cecil Stoughton, White House Photographs, John F. Kennedy Presidential Library and Museum, Boston, were a benefit in illustrating chapters 5, 13, 15, and 18.

Thanks go to Christie Wright, nonfiction history author and acting president of the Park County Local History Archives, for help in finding historical facts and papers; and to the Park County Local History Archives in Fairplay, for its collection of historic photographs and documents.

Special thanks go to my family for their unending support, and everyone who bought or read my first book, *Historic Tales from Park County: Parked in the Past.* Your encouragement led to this second book.

And a final, unending thanks to my husband, Tom Van Dusen, for his help with the cover of this book and for his continued support. He's always there when I return to the present after exploring the past.

Introduction

South Park, at the geographic center of Colorado in Park County, is a high-elevation mountain valley about fifty miles long, north to south, and about thirty-five miles wide. The immense basin is framed by lofty peaks of the Rocky Mountains. In the 1860s, South Park attracted thousands of miners looking for wealth in the Colorado gold rush. Over a century and a half later, its lures to worldwide visitors include outdoor recreation, wildlife, and the history of the Western frontier. The stories in this book reveal some of South Park's rich history.

With some modifications, the majority of the chapters in this book were first published in 2013 and 2014 in a monthly feature called "Parked in the Past" for the *Park County Republican and Fairplay Flume.* The Antero Reservoir chapter was first published in the June 2015 issue of *Colorado Central Magazine,* and the remaining chapters have not been previously published.

The first edition of the *Fairplay Flume* newspaper was issued on February 20, 1879. Its rival, the *Park County Republican,* began in 1912, and the two merged in 1918 to become the *Park County Republican and Fairplay Flume.* References in this book to the *Flume* apply throughout all of the newspaper's name changes.

Prehistory

Chapter 1

Porcupine Cave

Ancient South Park History

It was once proposed that South Park be designated the nation's largest wildlife refuge. The purpose was to "preserve one of Colorado's natural beauty hotspots, provide a sanctuary for all types of native game, and furnish a playground for the entire United States," said Governor Edwin C. Johnson in 1936.

The proposal didn't make it past the planning stage, but that doesn't change the fact that wildlife thrives in South Park, and, according to evidence found in an ancient Park County cave, it's been that way for at least one and a half million years.

Ice Age

Porcupine Cave, hidden inside a sagebrush-and-pine-covered hillside in a remote area of South Park, tells the story. It has attracted nationwide interest for the number and diversity of animal fossils from the Middle Pleistocene Ice Age found inside. It once held a menagerie of rodents and rabbits, mammals and birds, snakes, and even a cutthroat trout. They all made their way into Porcupine Cave an estimated one and a half million to three hundred thousand years ago. Their fossilized bones and scat hold clues to South Park's ancient past.

In all, the remains of 127 animal species were found in 26 locations inside the three-tiered cave, including 2 amphibians, 4 reptiles, 48 birds, and 73 mammals, according to the 2004 book *Biodiversity Response to Climate Change in the Middle Pleistocene: The Porcupine Cave Fauna from Colorado.*

The book is a collection of scientists' reports from research done from 1985 through 2000, edited and partially written by Anthony Barnosky, PhD.

At this writing, Barnosky is professor of integrative biology and curator at the Museum of Paleontology, University of California, Berkeley and was involved in much of the research in Porcupine Cave, first as a vertebrate paleontologist at Pittsburgh's Carnegie Museum and later with UC-Berkeley.

In his book, Barnosky said the cave is "arguably the richest source of information in the world on Irvingtonian-age vertebrates [animals living during the middle part of the Ice Age]." Ten years later his opinion hadn't changed. Contacted in 2014, Barnosky said Porcupine Cave is still one of the world's most important Ice Age sites.

Investigating Mark's Sink, site of the oldest fossils found in Porcupine Cave. *Photo courtesy of Larry Coats, Department of Geography, University of Utah.*

In the cave, researchers discovered the remains of the first known appearance of thirty-four animals and birds that still exist in South Park today, including the common raven, black-billed magpie, Wyoming ground squirrel, and two species of cottontail rabbit.

Rodent remains, specifically those of voles and wood rats (also known as packrats), were the most common fossils found inside the cave and ranged in age from the oldest fossil finds (one and a half million years old) to the newest (three hundred thousand years old). Because of that, scientists have been able to trace changes in the two as they evolved in the 1.2 million-year ancient history of the cave.

Animals

Porcupine Cave existed through varied climates of glacial (frozen) and interglacial (thawing) periods; consequently, some animals that lived in South Park during the Ice Age are not native to the area today. Evidence shows the musk ox lived in South Park during the glacial periods, and extinct species of the camel, ground sloth, and cheetah were in the area during the interglacial periods.

The ground sloth was one of the largest animals that lived in or near the cave. It could grow to a maximum of ten feet long and weigh as much as two tons; it resembled a large bear. Additionally, ancient coyote fossils dating from the cave's beginnings have been found. One severely deteriorated fossil shows evidence that the animal met death when its skull was crushed by the bite of another coyote in what was a literal dog-eat-dog world.

Scientists believe that some animals lived and raised their young in the cave; in fact, remains of two cheetah kittens were found inside. Other species that may have denned in the cave were coyotes, wolves, foxes, and bears. The ground sloth was a cave dweller, as were rodents. Wood rat nests and middens (piles of seeds, bones, and leaves) were found in the deep recesses of the cave.

Some animals were dragged inside by the twenty-two species of carnivores that lived in or around the cave; smaller carnivores were the badger, marten, mink, and weasel. Larger species included the bobcat, wolverine, and extinct Edward's wolf. Examples of prey animals, some of whose fossilized bones showed evidence of being gnawed on, were mountain goats, peccaries (wild pigs), large and small horses, deer, pikas, marmots, rabbits, prairie dogs, and various species of squirrels. Certain animals whose remains were found in the cave may have entered by accident. Scientists speculate that a camel may have fallen from a sinkhole and couldn't get out.

Approximately three hundred thousand years ago, shifting changes in the earth closed all entrances to the cave. The constant fifty-degree temperature preserved the fossils, and Porcupine Cave existed, unknown, until the 1860s.

Wyoming ground squirrels have lived in South Park for over 300,000 years. *Photo by the author.*

Discovery

Beginning in 1859, the Colorado gold rush attracted thousands of miners to South Park, and by the 1870s, silver was also being mined. Speculation is that sometime within the two decades, miners dug with picks and shovels into a hillside colored red with iron oxide—a sign that gold and silver might be nearby, according to Barnosky. They broke through a top layer of rock and dirt to discover the ancient cave layered with the remains of Ice Age animals. Scientists can only guess when miners first opened the cave, but the year 1890 was written in candle smoke in an area called "The Pit," so named because a ladder was required for access.

On August 3, 1923, Porcupine Cave was mentioned in a local newspaper— Buena Vista's *Chaffee County Republican*. The story told about a group of tourists, mostly from Park County, who visited the cave with area homesteader James M. Eubanks. The cave was described by the group as having amazing stalactites and stalagmites of "resplendent colors," and they said it was more wonderful and far larger than the Cave of the Winds near Colorado Springs. The following year, a report about Porcupine Cave appeared in South Carolina's December 24, 1924, *Spartanburg Herald*. It also said the cave rivaled Cave of the Winds and that, after further exploration, Porcupine Cave would become a national monument.

Barnosky disagreed that the cave had magnificent decorations. He said in his book that Porcupine Cave may have had some sparse decorations in the 1920s, but, if it did, those had long since disappeared by the 1980s.

On July 24, 1925, the *Chaffee County Republican* reported that a government surveyor, a Mr. Bradshaw, had worked at the cave for three weeks, accompanied by Eubanks. It reported the two had found an ivory tusk that, the story said, "must have belonged to some very large animal hundreds or thousands of years ago."

The *Republican* reported the cave "is a very fertile field for the work of scientists." Bradshaw's opinion, as reported by the *Republican*, was that "the world will be given new light on some forms of life that existed when this section was either the bed of an ocean or just after the Noah flood," and it said that the government was determined to see what kinds of animals lived in the cave in ages past.

Ownership Trail

The cave has only had three owners. A homestead claim was patented in February 1931 on the area surrounding the cave and sold a month later to a cattle rancher. The original homesteader kept easement rights to the cave with an option to purchase; his plans were apparently to develop it as a tourist attraction. The easement rights ran out in 1941, and the cave was not developed.

The rancher who was the second owner kept the land until 1962, when he passed ownership to another rancher. That rancher's family still owns the property.

Velvet Room

In 1939, two cowboys who worked for the second owner were riding by the cave, headed to a ranch rodeo. On a whim, they wrote a note, placed it in a Velvet-

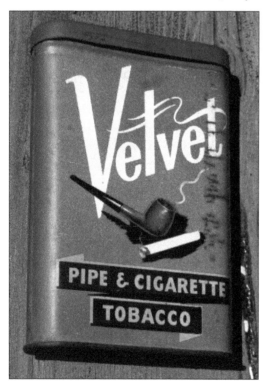

brand pipe and cigarette tobacco tin, and threw it in the cave entrance, like a message in a bottle—cowboy style. The note, dated June 14, from Lloyd Marshall and Elvis Conner, asked anyone who found the note to drop them a line. Included with their signatures were the towns where they lived, enough of an address for small towns of the day.

A 1939-era Velvet tobacco tin similar to this one was found in Porcupine Cave's Velvet Room in 1986. *Photo by the author.*

The tin was found forty-seven years later, in 1986, in the far reaches of the cave. It had been transported by a wood rat to its midden; that area was later named the Velvet Room. Spelunker Kirk Branson and oil geologist and paleontologist Don Rasmussen found the message and searched for the two cowboys. After phoning every Marshall and Conner living in the area of the cave, Branson eventually located Marshall living in Oregon. Conner was not found.

The tobacco-tin find was mentioned in a two-part story in the September 19 and September 26, 1986, issues of the *Fairplay Flume.* Reporter Stacy Bowman told about visiting the cave with *Flume* publisher Alberta Nelson and Barnosky, Branson, Rasmussen, and junior spelunker Zach McGuire. In the story, Branson said Marshall was really surprised when he was told the Velvet tin was found.

"At first he was skeptical, but when I read his words to him, he was thrilled," said Branson.

Modern Exploration

Recent discoveries at Porcupine Cave began in 1981, when Rasmussen and his 10-year-old son, Larry, were exploring in the area. On that trip, Larry found a fossilized horse tooth later confirmed to be from the Ice Age. Four years later, that discovery spurred a flurry of paleontological research (the study of what fossils tell us about the ecologies of the past, about evolution, and about our place, as humans, in the world).

The research began in 1985 and continued through the year 2000. Barnosky, Rasmussen, and other researchers from various institutions, including Pittsburgh's Carnegie Museum of Natural History, the Denver Museum of Natural History (later renamed Denver Museum of Nature and Science), and the University of California, Berkeley, began a research project to study the important historical treasure hidden at Porcupine Cave.

Note: Porcupine Cave is privately owned; access is by permission only.

1860s

Chapter 2

Montgomery City

Buried Boom Town

It was all "bustle and excitement" at Montgomery City when the September 24, 1861, *Rocky Mountain News* broke the story of a rich gold discovery there.

Montgomery City, Colorado, circa 1880s. *Park County Local History Archives, Special Collections, Colorado College, Colorado Springs.*

In a letter to the editor, the writer said the first claim was discovered in July 1861, and the new city was organized a month later, on August 22.

By the summer of 1862, there were two arrastras (early day pulverizing mills) in operation, another was nearly completed, and two twelve-stamp quartz mills were under construction. In one piece of quartz from the Allen Lode, at least twenty dollars in gold could be seen with the naked eye, and "half a pan of dirt from this land yielded $8," the *News* reported.

Comparing the value of gold in 1861–$18.93 per ounce–to the value on January 1, 2015–$1,206 per ounce–the rock would have been worth about $1,274 in early 2015, and the half pan of dirt would have been worth about $510. Eight other nearby claims were also reported to be "very rich," according to the *News* story.

Ninety-six years later, in 1957, a dam was completed, and the former site of Montgomery was buried under five thousand acre-feet of water. Montgomery Reservoir, near the summit of Hoosier Pass, serves as storage for Blue River water, diverted under the Continental Divide, and water from the Middle Fork of the South Platte River, flowing from its source above the former town. The water is owned by the City of Colorado Springs.

But in 1861, construction was in full swing on that late summer day, and no time was wasted in building. The writer told of putting up a cabin on the day he wrote to the *News.* He said, "Although I have only arrived here this morning, I have got part of my logs upon my lot, and will have a house ready for occupancy by day after tomorrow evening."

Grand plans were made in 1861 by the eleven founders of Montgomery. The plans they drew up for the new town included four sixty-foot-wide downtown streets running east to west–Main, Montgomery, Clinton, and Washington. Park Place, running from south to north near the middle of town, widened gradually as its course continued north from Washington. Two blocks later it ended at a large park situated between Montgomery and Main. Side streets were forty feet wide, lined with twenty-five-by-one-hundred-foot lots. The plans looked good on paper, but surviving photos tell a different story. The city was a jumble of buildings and structures thrown together without regard to the founders' design.

Montgomery grew fast. In 1861, two hotels were going up, and one was a two-story structure with dimensions of fifty feet by one hundred feet. It included a public hall on the top floor, where it is likely residents watched traveling shows.

Carroll's Minstrels played to full houses, alternating between Montgomery and Buckskin Joe, and theatrical groups entertained frequently in Montgomery.

One play, *The Soldier's Daughter*, was performed for Montgomery audiences in the spring or early summer of 1862. It was described as "a new and glorious comedy" in the April 3, 1862, *News*, boasting elegant wardrobes procured from New York and magnificent painted scenery. The Montgomery and Buckskin Joe showings were preceded by performances in Central City, Denver, and Georgia Gulch.

Reports of Montgomery's growth made the news throughout the fall and winter of its first year. A reporter described the booming town in the October 26, 1861, *News*. He said that four weeks earlier he had seen "the smoke curling from one solitary cabin, [and] there is now visible not less than fifty habitable abodes, and many of them quite large and roomy—beside a score more in process of erection."

The good news kept coming. From the November 5, 1861, *News*: "There is not as rich a region yet discovered."

Later editions told of gold-bearing quartz found at depths of less than twenty feet—said to be even richer than gold from the neighboring boomtown of Buckskin Joe (also called Laurette with various spellings). The gold at Montgomery was hard to get to, yet the prospectors kept digging.

"The deeper they sink," said the March 5, 1862, *News*, "the richer the quality of the quartz."

The names of the mines were as colorful as their yield. Among them were Pleasant Help, North Star, Magnolia, Vermont, Pocahontas, Little Thunder, and Woodchuck. Everyone wanted to get in on the action. The May 19, 1862, *News* reported five thousand claims within a one-mile radius of Montgomery.

Man's World

It was truly a man's world in early Montgomery and the entire South Park region, according to the 1860 US Census. The South Park enumeration district, part of Arapahoe County, Kansas Territory at the time, had three women residents. With the exception of three boys under age sixteen, the rest—or 10,437—were men, and over nine thousand of the men were miners aged twenty-one to forty. A nearby enumeration district called "Tarryall and South Park," was also predominantly male; there were nine women, nine children under sixteen, and 939 men.

Men of Montgomery, circa 1880. *Park County Local History Archives, James W. Nutt photo, Ed and Nancy Bathke Collection.*

Together in 1860, the two districts equaled 11,400 of the 32,049 living in Arapahoe County. Counting the total population of the future Colorado Territory (formed in 1861 from parts of Utah, New Mexico, Nebraska, and Kansas territories) the population of the two South Park districts equaled just under one third of Colorado's 34,277 total.

Probably the male-female ratio had not changed much by 1862, and that may have prompted the following singles ad published in the May 10, 1862, *News*. All he wanted was a well-mannered, affectionate young woman with lots of money.

> Wanted—A middle-aged gentleman, of pleasing address and moral manners, possessing several valuable gulch and lode claims in Buckskin Joe and Montgomery, is desirous of cultivating the acquaintance of some lady of accomplished manners and affectionate disposition, not over thirty-nine years of age, and with a view to matrimony and making a summer trip to Salmon River. She must be possessed of six or seven thousand dollars in dust [$382,250-$446,000 in January 2015 gold value] or Treasury notes [$140,000-$163,000 with inflation adjustment], so as to make assurance doubly sure, and enable the subscriber to devote his undivided attention to her and his travelling wants across the Utah Plains, and through the wild and rugged passes of the Snowy Range and Snake country. Address, in confidence, Z.Y.X., Denver, post office.

More Growth

In January 1862, with snow two feet deep, a third quartz mill was running. The region's greatest drawback was lack of workers, the *News* reported. With gold in abundance, deep snow did little to deter progress that year. In March 1862, Blake & Fay's store was doing a brisk business, and a third hotel, the two-story Exchange, opened.

"Buildings in every direction [were] rising as if tossed into existence by a magician's hand," said the March 24, 1862, *News*.

In May, two more hotels and two more stores opened, and in June, Alexander Ray opened a French bakery. Mail was delivered weekly in 1862, two daily stages ran between Montgomery and Buckskin Joe, and later in the year tri-weekly stages ran the entire one hundred miles to Denver, connecting Montgomery to the outside world. At about the same time, a Doctor Bailey came to Montgomery to open a medical practice and drug store. And if the *Fairplay Flume* of February 16, 1882, can be believed, he also preserved a human head in a pickle jar full of alcohol.

The story, written nineteen years after the incident, said in 1863 Doctor Bailey and others in a hunting party from Montgomery came upon the body of a man recently killed by Indians. Bailey, who had always wanted to study the anatomy of a human head, cut it off at the neck, took it to his office, placed it in the jar and kept it for several years.

Weather

Snow caused problems at times during Montgomery's boom years; the winter of 1863-1864 was especially tough, said Father John Dyer in his autobiography, *The Snow-Shoe Itinerant.* He said snowdrifts in Montgomery were to the tops of the doors and that, along the streets, steps were cut into the snow to access homes and businesses.

Another storm, described in Black Hawk's October 24, 1866, *Daily Mining Journal,* said snow began falling on October 10 at Montgomery. At noon the next day, forty inches had accumulated, and the snow was still falling.

Meanwhile

While the gold rush in Colorado brought settlers to Montgomery and other mining camps, back East "in the States," the Civil War was raging. The *News* reported daily on battles, but, as the South Park correspondent said, "The citizens of Park County glide along as smoothly and quietly as a duck in a storm."

It's not that people in Montgomery didn't know about the war. They did. For the most part residents supported the Union. In 1862, to show respect for the president, they named a nearby peak Mount Lincoln. At 14,286 feet, it is the highest peak in Park County and eighth highest in Colorado.

Indians were a worry whether they were fighting the settlers or other tribes. A story in the June 23, 1862, *News* reported a group of six hundred Indians (four hundred Arapaho and two hundred Sioux) were seen in Fairplay by Alex Ray, the Montgomery baker. It said they "were on a war expedition against the

Utes." During Montgomery's boom, residents were also watchful for outlaws, including the stage-robbing Reynolds Gang and the murderous Espinosa Brothers.

Decline

The first sign of Montgomery's decline was recounted in a January 13, 1865, *News* story of a mass meeting held by citizens of the Consolidated Montgomery Mining District. Mining was already depressed, and the meeting was held to find solutions. One problem was that claims at Montgomery were being made by individuals and corporations, some under fictitious names, who had no presence in the district, had made no improvements, and had not prospected on the claims—all required by law to prove a claim's validity. The unproven claims were being represented as legitimate lodes and were being sold to Eastern capitalists.

The fictitious claims were located throughout the district and were so close together that "it would be impossible for any new discovery to be made without coming in contact and conflict with one or more of those fictitious lodes," the *News* story said.

A resolution was passed at the meeting requiring all discoverers to "personally represent, or legally represent their interests in such mining property, at Montgomery City, Colorado, on or before the 15th day of March, A.D. 1865" to show their legal rights to hold the claims and show that necessary improvements had been made. If the requirements were not met, the claim would be declared vacant and all rights would be forfeited.

The resolution did little to stop Montgomery's downhill slide because the easily found rich ore near the surface was gone. Although mining continued for a while, digging deeper was costly. The November 22, 1867, *News* said there was talk of bringing in working capital from France to develop the mines.

New life came to Montgomery in the 1870s, when silver miners working claims on Mounts Bross and Lincoln commuted from Montgomery. That continued until 1893, when silver was demonetized, causing the price to plummet. By the early 1900s, tax liens and foreclosure sales were the only news from the former bonanza town.

Remains of unknown Montgomery residents were moved to this plot in the Fairplay Cemetery in 1953. *Photo by the author.*

Dammed

After lying dormant for more than fifty years, another change came to Montgomery. In July 1954, a bid was accepted by Fisher Contracting of Phoenix to build a dam at the former townsite. In the years between 1954 and 1957, when the dam was under construction, remaining structures that once defined the prosperous mining town were removed.

The twelve bodies buried in the small Montgomery cemetery were also moved. Grave markers had long since disappeared, and wooden caskets, if there had been any, had disintegrated. Remains of the earliest Montgomery citizens were collected and buried in a mass grave at the Fairplay cemetery. A single marker in the northeast corner of the grounds indicates the fenced site.

Today

Tranquil is what best describes the Montgomery area today. In summer and fall, anglers are drawn to the sounds of water lapping the rock-strewn shore and leaves rustling in the mountain breeze. An old road above the reservoir leads hikers, historians, and off-road buffs to the abandoned Magnolia Mill, and, about three and a half miles farther, to Wheeler Lakes. Winters are still harsh. Snow piles high, breezes change to chilling winds, and reservoir water freezes deep. As in the past, it is often late June before the winter thaw is over.

Montgomery Reservoir, 2014. *Photo by the author.*

Chapter 3

The Letters of Wilbur Fisk Stone

Tales of Merciless Outlaws and Dishonest Authorities in 1860s Colorado

Wilbur Fisk Stone made his mark in life as an editor, journalist, author, politician, and judge. But in the years from 1860 to about 1865, before his fame, he was a budding attorney and successful miner living in the South Park bonanza towns of Hamilton and Montgomery. He didn't have Pikes-Peak-or-Bust gold fever, he said at age eighty-four in a 1916 interview; he was simply in the territory to "look it over."

Letters he wrote during those years to his future bride, Sarah (or Sallie) Sadler—he called her Minnie—have survived for over a century and a half. Through the generosity of the Stone family, some of those letters were used for this story.

Justice Wilbur Fisk Stone served on the Colorado Supreme Court from 1877–1886. *Photo courtesy of Mark and Elizabeth Stone, descendants of Wilbur Fisk Stone, Williamson Photo, Denver.*

They give a firsthand account of the Colorado gold rush and that volatile time of merciless outlaws and alleged dishonest authorities in 1860s Colorado. The letters were meant for Minnie alone, and foremost in each is his testament of love for her. But within the letters are nuggets of Colorado history, written with the expectation that none but Minnie would read his words.

Stone's first political victory was in Park County, where, in December 1861, he was elected a territorial representative in the first election of the new Colorado Territory and, in 1863, reelected. In the field of law, he was judicial committee chairman of Colorado's 1875 Constitutional Convention (the group that wrote the draft of the constitution for Colorado pending its acceptance into the Union). During his lifetime, he was an assistant US district attorney, an attorney for the US Court of Private Land Claims, and the first attorney for the Denver and Rio Grande Railroad. In a statewide election in 1877, he was elected a justice on the Colorado Supreme Court by 99 percent of the voters. (He ran as a replacement to a justice who resigned after serving only a few months of a nine-year term. The nominating committee chose Stone unanimously, and he ran unopposed.)

As an author, Stone recorded histories of prominent Coloradans in a four-volume set titled *History of Colorado*. As a journalist, he was assistant editor of the *Nebraskan* (now *Omaha World-Herald*) and was first editor of the *Colorado Chieftain* (now the *Pueblo Chieftain*). In its first edition of June 1, 1868, he reported the death of the American explorer, scout, and trapper Kit Carson. He wrote numerous articles for territorial newspapers under the pen name "Dornick," a mid-19th century term meaning stone. One of those newspapers was the *Denver Weekly Commonwealth and Republican*. It later merged with the *Rocky Mountain News*.

His professional accomplishments are documented in books, magazines, journals, and Internet pages; his life in early South Park during the gold rush is less known. Only a few references were found in all the published records. The letters to Minnie and limited newspaper clips may be the only sources documenting his life in South Park.

Young Stone

In late April 1860, twenty-six-year-old Wilbur Fisk Stone arrived in Denver by wagon train. Originally from Connecticut, he was already an accomplished lawyer, writer, and editor. He was raised in Oskaloosa, Iowa; his trip west began from his then-home of Omaha, Nebraska.

Stone spent a few weeks in Denver before he set out for the Tarryall Diggings (consisting of Tarryall City and Hamilton, occupying opposite banks of Tarryall Creek), north of the site of today's Como. He wanted to see the gold fields and had plans to return to Omaha after a brief adventure. He ended up staying in Colorado for the rest of his life, another sixty years.

Stone was in Hamilton on Tuesday, July 10, 1860, when he wrote to Minnie, saying he missed her. He told her he carried the locket with her photo with him everywhere and that he opened it often to "look into those eyes and on that face which I know is true." He told Minnie the locket was "dearer to (him) than all the gold in the gulches."

Wilbur Fisk Stone, circa 1863, when he lived in Montgomery. *Photo courtesy of Mark and Elizabeth Stone, descendants of Wilbur Fisk Stone.*

Mining

Stone had a mining partnership with two other men in the summer of 1860; the three took turns going out looking for gold. One partner who left to prospect in mid-June never returned. After ten days, Stone sent the other partner out to find the first man. When the second partner returned to Hamilton two weeks later, he reported walking two hundred miles and finding no trace. Stone told Minnie he suspected the first partner had found a claim to keep for himself or had headed southwest and was scalped by Navajos. The scenario was not uncommon; in the Colorado Territory a man could easily disappear, never to be seen again.

While Stone was waiting to hear from the missing partner, he wrote to Minnie that his plans for the winter were uncertain. He hinted that he would come to Indiana (where she was) if she would just say the word. And he enclosed with the letter petals of alpine flowers that he had collected above timberline, "just below the line of habitual snow."

Bloody Espinosas

On Thursday, April 30, 1863, Stone was living in Montgomery when he wrote to Minnie, "We are in worse than a panic here just now. This country is overrun with guerrillas, bandits and outlaws so that it is no longer safe to travel."

He continued, "Five men have been murdered near here right in day light and in sight of town. These robbers secrete themselves in the mountain passes and woods and deliberately shoot down the unsuspecting passerby and then rob him . . . he is first shot down and then searched and if no money is found the murderers curse their luck and try another."

All of the stagecoaches and mail carriers were under heavy escort, and Stone himself volunteered as an escort. He said, "It is terrible, this constant looking, watching and fearing at every turn the deadly assassin who in a moment sends you into eternity with all your imperfections on your head." Stone said that during these times, stagecoach passengers were "all armed from head to foot (with) a cavalry escort of six soldiers."

Possibly to assure Minnie, he said the hope was that soon the outlaws would be cleared out of the country. And he told her not to worry that he would be drafted into the Civil War.

He wrote:

> There will be no draft here in Colorado, this is the opinion of all both
> military and civil men, for these reasons: We have now in the field
> more than our quota of volunteers; there have been no desertions to
> speak of; the (regiments) are full in the field; there is danger all
> round us as a territory; prospects of a Mormon war in Utah adjoining;
> Indians on all sides of us; threatened invasions from Texas and New
> Mexico; guerrillas overrunning the country, and our population
> decimated by enlistments and emigration to the new mines so that
> no more men can be spared from this territory. They are needed here
> for domestic protection. So, Dearest, you need have no fear of my
> being drafted.

The guerrillas, bandits, and outlaws Stone wrote about included two
brothers—Felipe and Vivian Espinosa—who came from what was then northern
Mexico and is now near Taos in the state of New Mexico. Historians have called
the brothers the "Bloody Espinosas" for their merciless and senseless killing
spree. Felipe, first with Vivian and later with Jose Espinosa, murdered and
mutilated an estimated thirty-two people from late 1862 through October 1863
in Colorado, including five victims buried in the Old Fairplay Cemetery. The
reign of terror subsided somewhat in June 1863, when Vivian Espinosa was
captured and killed.

But Felipe wasn't done yet. According to Vivian's diary, the killing spree was
to avenge the death of six family members slain in the Mexican-American War
(1846–1848). The brothers planned to murder 100 people for each of their
relatives killed in the war. In early October 1863, Felipe recruited his fourteen-
year-old nephew, Jose. The spree continued until October 15, when Felipe and
Jose were ambushed, killed, and beheaded by army scout Tom Tobin at their
campsite near Fort Garland in south-central Colorado.

Indian Wars

Stone's background in journalism and politics put him in direct knowledge of
government actions and events that occurred in the fall of 1864. In a letter dated
September 9, he told Minnie, "I have been behind the curtain [seen the truth],

Minnie, and I am sick of hypocrisy in the blue clothes of patriotism, and knavery [unprincipled, dishonest trickery] in shoulder straps."

His letter was dated just eleven weeks before the notorious Sand Creek Massacre, when on November 29-30, 1864, the Colorado militia under the command of Colonel John Chivington attacked and destroyed a village of Cheyenne and Arapaho Indians camped on Sand Creek in southeastern Colorado. The letter tells of events leading up to the carnage.

Stone didn't mention the men by name in his letter, but he told Minnie about corruption, lying, and thievery by the military commander of the territory (Chivington) and said the governor (Governor John Evans, who was also superintendent of Indian affairs) had been involved in corruption. Evans and Chivington kept the public informed of both Indian warfare and the army's retaliation to it, and, according to Stone, they didn't always tell the truth.

He said, "I have seen thirty-thousand dollars stolen from the government by a Methodist preacher wearing shoulder straps." (It seems likely Stone was referring to Chivington, who was a presiding elder of the Methodist church when he first came to Denver in 1860. He was offered a chaplain's commission when he joined the Army in 1862 but chose a fighting appointment instead.)

The letter continued:

> I have seen the military commander of the territory cause it to be published and proclaimed on the streets that a widow and two accomplished daughters had been murdered and scalped at their ranch a few miles from Denver, by the Indians the day before, when he knew at the time it was a lie; that the family were alive and well, and more, that not an Indian had been within forty miles of there for a month.
>
> I have seen a major sent out on the plains to fight Indians, who was gone three weeks, came upon two lone friendly Indians unarmed who were herding horses, approach them under the guise of friendship and brutally murder these two defenseless Indians, steal the whole herd of horses, sell them along the road and put the money in his pockets and those of his men, make out the official report to the commandant at Denver that he had in a great fight killed 40 hostile Indians, and bribe the commandant by a present of two Indian ponies to confirm the report.

I have seen this same loyal and self-sacrificing military commander together with the governor and quartermaster let a hay contract to their friends by which one hundred thousand dollars' profit was made and the sum divided with the officials. Men who speak of these things, I have seen denounced for it as copperheads [Southern sympathizers]. And this is a free country; a pure government that devoutly asks God to be on its side. No wonder the war does not end.

The incidents could not be verified.

Wilbur Stone closed this letter by describing how pleasant it was to be in Montgomery. Days were sunny, nights were cool, berries were ripe for the picking, and the fish were biting. Wilbur's thoughts, when not on corruption in government, were on Minnie and how he wanted to see her again.

He ended with, "God bless you, Dearest, is my prayer every day and night and speed the day when our future may be as happy in reality as it has been in anticipation. I kiss you good night, Love, and may angels carry it to you in dreams."

Wilbur and Minnie were married in February 1866 in Bloomington, Indiana; shortly after the marriage, they began their life together in Pueblo, Colorado.

Note: Two spellings were found for Wilbur Stone's middle name, one with an "e" on the end—Fiske—and one without an "e", which is the spelling used in this chapter. I chose to use the same spelling as in the historic versions of his books, History of Colorado, Volumes 1-4; as on his headstone at Denver's Fairmount Cemetery; and as on the website, http://judgestone.com/home.html, maintained by his ancestors, Mark and Elizabeth Stone.

1870s

Chapter 4

Fairplay Hotel History Unfolds at Fifth and Main

Louis Valiton and Abraham Bergh– First Owners

I t's hard to imagine the thousands of people who have walked through the doors of the hotels at Fifth and Main in Fairplay since 1873. It's been a revolving door of miners and marshals, tourists and travelers, society couples and cowboys—a cross section of humanity representing all walks of life for almost a century and a half.

Two structures have occupied that site. The first, built by Louis Valiton in 1873, originally carried his name. Later it was operated as the McLean House, the Bergh House, the Vestel House, a second round as the Bergh House, and, last, the Hotel Windsor under two owners. That hotel burned to the ground in 1921.

Fairplay-Valiton Hotel in December 2015. *Photo by the author.*

In 1922, the larger, more elegant, and still-existing Fairplay Hotel opened. (In 2010, the hotel was renamed the Fairplay-Valiton.) Since opening, it has been the community social center and *the* place to go for dances, meetings, and, from 1971 through 1973, dinner theater productions. Famed guests included entertainer Bob Hope and prizefighter Jack Dempsey.

The full history of hotels at Fifth and Main would be a book in itself; following is a brief history of two early owners—both were born in 1835, accomplished much, and died young.

Valiton

As an adult, Louis Frederick Valiton was tall, lanky, blue-eyed, and bearded, according to an aged 1873 photograph and family information on ancestry.com. The family believes he suffered from epilepsy; possibly that condition contributed to his early death.

An 1873 faded photo of Valiton's wife, Maria Catherine Valiton, shows her to be about five feet seven inches tall, with a small waist and long dark hair worn in ringlets.

Louis Valiton was born in France in June 1835. At age seventeen, in 1852, he immigrated to New Orleans, and from there moved to Dubuque, Iowa, where, in 1858, he married Maria Catherine Ferney, also from France. Louis was the first of her four husbands.

Move West

The newlyweds lived in Missouri, where their first son, Charles, was born on June 6, 1859. Two years later, they began a westward journey, leaving St. Joseph, Missouri, on May 1, 1861. They traveled the Smoky Hill trail in "a covered wagon drawn by two spans of mules," said a 1925 Charles Valiton story, "Forty-Five Years in Colorado." A copy of the publication is available at the Park County Local History Archives.

The Valitons were following the "Pikes Peak gold excitement," said Charles Valiton. Along the way they had help from the Sioux, Cheyenne, and Arapaho Indians, who "were friendly to the whites and kept the emigrants well supplied with fresh buffalo and venison in exchange for flour, sugar, tobacco and coffee." Six weeks later, on June 15, 1861, the family arrived in Denver.

(The Valitons were probably fortunate that they traveled early in the 1860s decade. Indian uprisings increased on the Great Plains as the 1860s wore on, culminating in the American Indian Wars of 1866–1890.)

Park County

In 1862, Louis Valiton was a justice of the peace in Georgia Gulch, Summit County, Colorado Territory. In 1864, the family was living in Montgomery City when a second son, Delore, was born on August 25. While there, Valiton was secretary of the Consolidated Montgomery Mining District and postmaster for the town.

The family moved in about 1867 to Fairplay, where Louis Valiton was an agent for a stagecoach line and ran Valiton's Drug Store. The store had a large inventory of drugs and medicines and also sold an assortment of general merchandise, "fancy articles" (luxury items), wines, and liquors, according to an advertisement in the September 28, 1868, *Rocky Mountain News*. The family welcomed a newborn daughter in 1869 when Leontine (or Lenora) was born in Fairplay.

The couple's oldest son, Charles Valiton, became a printer and journalist who wrote for several Colorado newspapers in the early part of the 1900s. He occasionally left that profession and mined, but he always came back to writing. In the 1920s, he was a police officer in Seattle, yet he still sent Colorado news tips to his former colleagues in the state. In the December 9, 1910, *Flume*, he authored a story about the years his father operated the drugstore in Fairplay.

In that story, he said Chief Saguache of the Ute tribe, a large man at five feet ten inches tall and about 240 pounds, visited Valiton's Drug Store. Charles Valiton remembered the whole tribe visiting when he was a small boy and said he made a long friendship with the chief by giving candy and nuts to his three squaws and their young papooses.

In Charles Valiton's words, "The Indians traded buckskins, buffalo robes and beaver, [and] bear and mountain lion skins for flour, coffee, sugar and canned goods, also for flashy colored calicos for their squaws." He said the tribe would camp near Fairplay for several days at a stretch.

In 1873, Louis Valiton built the first hotel at what is now the corner of Fifth and Main Streets in Fairplay.

Sale of Hotel

Within a year, Maria Valiton began to place weekly advertisements in the *Rocky Mountain News*, offering the hotel for sale or rent.

"A new hotel on Front street, opposite the Court House square, Fairplay, Colorado," the ad said. The main building was two stories high, with twenty rooms and a seven-room, one-story addition.

The hotel was probably for sale due to Louis Valiton's health. He died in 1875, at the age of thirty-nine, leaving his wife, age forty-three, to raise the children: Charles, fifteen, Delore, eleven, and Lenora, six. The property was sold in 1874 or 1875.

A mention in the February 25, 1898, *Flume* tells of a visit to Fairplay by Elizabeth McLean. The Flume said, "It has been many years since she was here but she will be remembered by some as the first landlady of the McLean House, later known as the Bergh House." From this it is apparent that McLean owned the hotel between ownership by Valiton and Bergh.

Three More Marriages

After her husband's death, Maria Catherine Valiton moved to Animas City, Colorado, a historic town now absorbed within the city limits of Durango. In 1880, at age forty-eight, she married Frank DesChamps. They apparently divorced. Information on ancestry.com shows that by 1890 DesChamps was married to another woman and living in New Mexico. He died there in 1910.

Maria Catherine DesChamps, age fifty, was living in Durango in 1882 when she and Nicholas Bergstrand were married. He left on a mining trip to Arizona on April 10, 1884. When he didn't return by October, Maria placed an advertisement on the front page of Flagstaff's October 18, 1884, *Arizona Champion*, asking for information on her husband's whereabouts. She described Nicholas Bergstrand as about forty-three years old, five feet five inches tall, with light sandy hair and light gray eyes. He had a moustache and beard, was Norwegian by birth, and spoke broken English. He was last seen in the company of three men at Fort Wingate, New Mexico. He was never found.

Back in Animas City, Maria Catherine Bergstrand apparently had the missing Nicholas declared dead. In 1901, when Maria was sixty-nine years old, she married for a fourth time to Mathew Salmhofer. He preceded her in death by a few months in 1910, when she was seventy-eight years old.

Bergh

Abraham Bergh was born in Milwaukee in 1835. He came to Colorado in 1859 when he was twenty-four, and married Lena Evans in 1862. They had seven children; three died in childhood. Bergh was appointed as the postmaster at Buckskin Joe in 1868 and was reappointed in 1872. It is uncertain if the family ever lived in Buckskin, but they were living in Fairplay by 1870. Abraham (or Abram) was a thirty-four-year-old miner. He lived with his wife, Lena, then thirty-one; daughters Lucy, six, and Mary, four; and one-year-old son Burton.

In November 1874, the Masons established Fairplay's Doric Lodge No. 25 (still existing in 2016), and Abraham Bergh was its first worshipful master (W.M.), or master of the lodge. (The term "worshipful master" is one of respect, used in the same way one would address a judge as "your honor.") He completed four terms as W.M. and died during his fifth term in 1892.

The Bergh House operated at Fifth and Main from 1876–1879 and again from 1880–1892. *Park County Local History Archives, T. C. Miller photo, Ed and Nancy Bathke Collection.*

Abraham Bergh bought the hotel in late 1876 and renamed it the Bergh House. One of the first advertisements Bergh placed for his hotel was simple and to the point: "The Bergh house at Fairplay, Colorado, is the only first-class house in the place. A. Bergh, Proprietor." It appeared in the December 6, 1876, *Colorado Mountaineer*, published in Colorado Springs.

In 1879, Bergh was the president of the Fairplay town board. He served with other town notables, such as John Hoover (he was lynched from a second floor window of the Park County courthouse in 1880), Joe Summer (he owned and operated saloons in Fairplay and Como and died by suicide in 1883), and Park County Sheriff John Ifinger.

Success

The year 1879 was a productive one for Bergh. The hotel was doing so well that in April a thirty-room addition was added, and in May a self-supporting circular staircase became part of the décor. The hotel welcomed notable guests such as Horace Tabor, Ulysses S. Grant Jr. (the former president's son), and John L. Routt.

At the time, Routt was Colorado's governor. He was the first to hold the position following Colorado's admittance to the Union and served four years, from 1876 through 1879. He also served from 1891 through 1893 as the state's seventh governor. In between governorships, he was mayor of Denver from 1883 to 1885.

The Bergh House was sold in August 1879, and the family moved to Denver. It was bought by E. N. Marsh and was called the Vestel House.

Heartbreak

Later that year, the Berghs suffered the worst blow that any parent can imagine. They had unknowingly moved to Denver in the midst of a typhoid fever outbreak; it lasted from the summer of 1879 through the end of 1880. Four of their children were infected.

Mary Josephine, called Mamie, died on November 28, 1879. She was described in the December 4, 1879, *Flume* as a "bright, loveable girl of fourteen summers, whose gentle manners and disposition had endeared her to all."

Burton was eleven years old when he died eleven days after his sister, on December 9, 1879. While Mamie died in her sleep, the *Flume* reported that Burton "suffered very much." The story in the December 11, 1879, *Flume* said that Burton's sister, Etta, then eight, was improving. She survived.

Abbie, age four, was the fourth Bergh child to develop typhoid fever. She died in late December 1879 when the family was traveling through Kansas City on the way to Abraham Bergh's Milwaukee birthplace.

Healing

In June 1880, the Berghs were still living in Denver with their two surviving children, Lucy, sixteen, and Etta, nine. The following month, Abraham Bergh repurchased the hotel at Fifth and Main—then called the Vestel House—and changed the name back to the Bergh House. It was still a first-class hotel; it was also a place for those injured in mines or fires to convalesce.

Etta Bergh, age seventeen, is part of a Fairplay Sunday school class in 1888. She is standing, second from left, in the back row. *Park County Local History Archives, Philip A. McKee family.*

Life for the Berghs was improving. Abraham Bergh was elected mayor of Fairplay on August 31, 1880, the family welcomed eleven-pound newborn son John on November 12, 1880, and two hundred-plus guests enjoyed the Masonic ball at the Bergh House on December 27, 1880. A daughter, Elizabeth, was born into the family in 1883.

Bergh's political aspirations grew past the town of Fairplay. He served in the Colorado House of Representatives from 1881 through 1886. While he was there, he introduced a bill to "prevent fraud upon hotel and boarding house keepers," said the January 20, 1881, *Flume*.

Fever

Typhoid fever struck the Bergh home again in late August 1892, infecting Abraham. He was confined to bed for several weeks in September and October, even as he was appointed Park County's representative to the Republican convention. He was too ill to serve.

By mid-September the family wanted to bring Abraham to Denver for treatment as soon as he could be moved; the *Flume* reported he was "irrational a good deal of the time." Dr. Frank Perigo, Bergh's nephew, came from Milwaukee to treat his ailing uncle. Bergh kept getting weaker; he was not moved to Denver.

On October 27, 1892, the *Flume* reported other members of the family were ill with typhoid, including twelve-year-old John. Abraham was reported to be "somewhat on the gain."

John survived, but Abraham Bergh, fifty-seven, lost his life on October 29 at his home in Fairplay. His remains were taken to Denver by train and stored in a vault until the family was well enough to attend a Masonic ceremony and burial.

Sale

Following Abraham Bergh's death, the Bergh House was leased to two gentlemen with surnames Radford and Wright; they ran the Radford House Hotel on Front Street and used the Bergh House as an annex. In February 1897, the hotel was sold to N. W. and Susannah Harris Young, who did extensive renovations and opened it as the Hotel Windsor.

Note: Typhoid symptoms include fever, severe headache, nausea, loss of appetite, constipation, diarrhea, and general discomfort. In the days before public sanitation, contents of cesspools and privies escaped into the soil and contaminated the earth and water, causing typhoid fever outbreaks. Antibiotics will cure most cases; however, the first antibiotic, penicillin, was discovered in 1928—too late for the Bergh family.

Chapter 5

Stagecoaches

Mass Transit in the Nineteenth Century

Drivers on today's Park County roads take nearly the same routes nineteenth-century stagecoaches took and see some of the same scenery. But that's where the similarities end.

It's an annoyance to modern travelers when the car breaks down, when traffic delays eat into busy schedules, or when dirt and gravel side roads turn to washboards. Travel in a stagecoach would put our modern discomfort into perspective. It was no joy ride.

The mud-wagon stagecoach shown above is the same type used throughout South Park from the 1860s into the 1920s. *Photo courtesy of Wikimedia Commons Public Domain.*

With a top speed of ten miles per hour on the flat and a more common speed of five miles per hour, the ninety-mile ride from Denver to Fairplay on the stagecoach took sixteen to eighteen hours and required an overnight stay. According to advertisements in the *Rocky Mountain News* of 1873, the fare was $12, equivalent to about $235 in 2015 dollars.

Seating

Because of the seating arrangement, one couldn't help but become acquainted with fellow travelers. The Abbot Downing Company's large overland wagon, the stagecoach model most often used in the mountainous West, had an inside space of about forty-five inches wide and sixty-five inches long, and its inside height was seven to eight feet.

Nine passengers sat in three rows; each traveler occupied a fifteen-inch-square leather seat, and had about seven inches of legroom. In comparison, the width of coach-class airline seats today is up to five inches wider, with legroom five times greater, according to CNN Travel at www.cnn.com.

The front row faced backward; the middle and back seats faced forward. Passengers in the front and middle seats, facing each other, had to dovetail their knees in order to fit; passengers sitting on the ends had to brace one leg against the window or hang their leg out the door. Another discomfort for passengers in the middle row was that they had no backrest. Foot space was determined by the number of packages, pieces of luggage, and mail sacks that didn't fit in the front and back boot and were stored on the floor of the passenger section.

According to a story by Doug Hansen in the July 2009 *Cowboys and Indians* magazine, the best passenger seat on a stagecoach, at least in good weather, was sitting next to the driver. That seat, called the box, had space for three. It was eight feet off the ground, and the passenger had an impressive view of the countryside while watching the driver control six running horses by the three reins he held in each hand. An express agent rode shotgun, also in the box. His job was to guard gold shipments and currency. One or two bench seats, holding three passengers each, were on top of the stage, behind the box.

The Chinaman's seat, with room for four, was a loose board between leather straps, facing backward on the back of the stage. The slang term originated because it was common for Chinese workers to sit back there. These seats had the lowest fare, and passengers were breathing dust the entire ride.

Once passengers, packages, and freight were arranged, a team of six horses or mules sped to the next stop, ten to twelve miles away. It was a ride of at least an hour, more commonly two.

Some comforts were built into stagecoach design. There were leather strap braces between the coach and undercarriage, making it swing from side to side during travel instead of jolting up and down. Mark Twain described the stagecoach as a "cradle on wheels" in his 1872 travel book, *Roughing It.* At each stop, a new team was harnessed, and passengers could stretch, use restrooms, and get a bite to eat. Food was generally what could be cooked fast or was premade—coffee, beans, bacon, and hard biscuits. A better meal was served at overnight stops for as little as fifty cents (about $9.50 in 2015 dollars).

In 1870, stages were scheduled "tri-weekly from Denver to Hamilton, Fairplay and the South Park Country," an ad in the November 16, 1870, *Rocky Mountain News* advised. The stage left Denver on Mondays, Thursdays, and Saturdays. (Hamilton no longer exists. It was about two miles northwest of Como on Tarryall Creek, site of the first gold discovery in Park County.)

Traffic

Reports in the *Flume* indicate stages were common in Park County. The April 3, 1879, edition reported a full load of passengers on every Alma stage, and the July 2, 1885, issue reported four stages daily to the mining town of Montgomery. In the April 1, 1880, *Flume,* the Pioneer Stage Company advertised two stages running daily from Como to "Breckinridge" in three hours, making connections with all trains running east and west.

(The paragraph above shows the old spelling of Breckenridge. The original spelling, in 1859, was "Breckinridge," after then US Vice President John Breckinridge. The town's spelling was changed in 1861 by citizens outraged when Breckinridge joined the Confederacy, according to www.blog.breckenridge.com. The *Flume* was still using the original spelling in 1880.)

Even as late as 1904, the Spotswood & McClelland line ordered five new Concord stages for the Fairplay-to-Leadville route, and "the stages were all crowded," according to station agent A. B. Crook in the April 1, 1904, *Flume.*

Accidents

Statistics weren't found on the number of stagecoach accidents in Park County, and few were reported happening. One that occurred four miles south of Wellington Lake in neighboring Jefferson County on July 27, 1902, resulted in the death of a Denver city alderman (elected member of a city council); another passenger was seriously injured. The two were with other Denver officials and three newspapermen on a trip to investigate the Denver water supply at Cheesman Reservoir.

The stage lurched suddenly, causing the driver to lose control. He was thrown from his seat, and the horses ran wildly down the mountain. Alderman Andrew Kelly, sitting in front with the driver, sustained fatal injuries. He tried to grab the reins and fell over the front of the stage.

"His forehead was crushed and he sustained a rupture," said the August 1, 1902, *Flume.*

City Committee Supervisor Carl M. Lindquist, weighing about three hundred pounds, jumped from the stage and landed on his left foot. That leg broke on impact.

"The front bone [tibia], which was dislocated, was forced through the skin," the *Flume* reported.

Robberies

Seemingly more common than accidents were robberies by masked bandits. One reported in Boulder's April 11, 1895, *Daily Camera* told of two men who robbed the Cripple Creek stage, making away with $16,000 in currency and $1,000 in gold.

They flagged down the four-horse stage two miles from town and asked for a ride. One man sat with driver Robert Smith; the other sat behind Smith. The man behind Smith hit him on the head with a revolver, the other hit Smith with a fist. Smith was dazed. After rifling the mail sacks, the two cut out the lead horses and escaped. Smith managed to drive with the remaining horses to Cripple Creek before he fainted.

Six weeks later, on May 28, 1895, the *Leadville Herald Democrat* reported the capture of two men in Leadville who were responsible for the Cripple Creek stage robbery and other crimes. Arrested were Stewart "Kid" Gray and Samuel Starr, "of the notorious Starr gang," the *Herald Democrat* reported.

"They are bad men," said Captain F. J. Dodge of Kansas City, special officer with Wells, Fargo & Company's Express "and your sheriff has made a big catch."

(Wells, Fargo & Company provided banking services and speedy transportation—express—of gold and other valuables across the country by Pony Express, railroad, and stagecoach.)

Whips

Stage drivers were called Jehus, after the Biblical Jehu—a fast and furious driver—and whips, possibly because they all carried one. They were greatly respected and were known to treat others with respect. Whips typically dressed in a long linen duster coat (to keep off dust, rain, and wind); long leather gloves; a wide-brimmed, low-crowned felt hat; and tall leather boots.

One whip in Park County was Perley Wason (or Wasson). Born in about 1845 in Vermont, he was eighteen when he started driving stages, first probably in Wisconsin, where he was raised, and later in the Dakotas. In 1873, he began driving stages in South Park for Spotswood & McClelland. When that firm received a shipment of new Concord stages in May 1879, one had the name "Perley" painted on it to honor Wason.

The *Flume* of May 20, 1879, reported that Wason "is without a doubt the most careful and fortunate driver in the West, having never met with a serious accident in all of his 17 years of staging." The story continued:

> To know that Perley holds the reins is security enough for any of the thousands who, having ridden with him once, have occasion to go over the road again. Steady, industrious and honest as the day is long, he is held in the highest esteem by his employers and all of his acquaintances and is a man to be selected from a thousand of his fellows.

In 1880, Wason ran a livery and stage service in Leadville. Two years later, he was the postmaster of Meserole, Colorado, thirty-five miles northwest of Durango in La Plata County. In 1883, he ran the halfway house between Dolores and Rico, Colorado, and, from 1889 to 1891, he was appointed by

Governor Job Adams Cooper as the first sheriff of Colorado's Montezuma County.

After 1891, Wason was running a stage and livery service in Cortez, Colorado, and having financial troubles. As train tracks were laid to more towns, railroads took over mail delivery contracts from stagecoaches, and stage businesses suffered. In 1892, Wason lost his home, stage outfit, and horses when the Montezuma Valley Bank of Cortez repossessed his property, according to the *Cortez Journal* of November 3, 2012. It revealed the news in the story, "Perley Wason, business pioneer," an article looking back at the old days, written by Dale Davidson of the Montezuma Historical Society.

Wason later moved to Rifle, Colorado. He died and was buried there in 1914.

Restored mud-wagon at South Park City Museum in Fairplay, Colorado. *Photo by the author.*

South Park Stages

By 1874, passengers rode the train as far as Morrison before completing the trip to Fairplay by stage. In July 1878, train tracks were completed to Bailey's Ranch (now called Bailey), and in the summer of 1879, the Denver, South Park and Pacific Railroad topped Kenosha Pass and established stations at Jefferson, Como, and Garo. Stages were still used into the early 1920s for travel to and from train depots. Their use died out when automobiles became popular.

Mosquito Pass Stage

The Mosquito Pass Road was completed in July 1879, and on July 23 the first tolls were taken.

"Over 150 outfits passed over the road that day," said the July 24, 1879, *Flume.*

According to the *Flume*, the stage station on Mosquito Pass "is likely to become quite a town." A store and saloon were under construction, and lumber was on order for a large hotel. Stables were being built for four stage companies—Spotswood & McClelland, Wall & Watter, Matthew McLaughlin's Stage Line, and the Despatch Company (probably a reference to the Butterfield Overland Despatch Company, better known for traveling the Smoky Hill Trail from Atchison, Kansas, to Denver. It also serviced the Colorado mountains).

The *Flume* said, "The general idea prevails that the road [Mosquito Pass] will be kept open the year around."

As of mid-2016, that still hasn't happened, but the hotel was built.

A notice in the July 8, 1880, *Flume*, announced the Half-Way House hotel's opening on June 12, 1880, by owner James Minihan. In the late 1950s, that same hotel was moved to Fairplay's South Park City Museum and is on display as the Stage Coach Inn.

Also at the museum is the cosmetically restored large overland wagon stagecoach, originally built by the Abbot Downing Company of Concord, New Hampshire. It is the type of stage that ran the circle route from Fairplay to Alma, over Mosquito Pass to Leadville, on to Salida, and back to Fairplay.

Stage stop in Mosquito Gulch on the east side of Mosquito Pass. *Park County Local History Archives.*

When looking at rough roads still existing in Park County, one can easily imagine the overland stage rushing alongside a creek, pulled by a team of well-trained and matched horses bringing miners, government officials, and schoolteachers to a new home in the Colorado Rockies. Think of those who settled the land the next time traffic is stopped on the highway. Think of them zipping across the prairie at ten miles per hour, crowded inside or hanging on for dear life on the top of a stagecoach.

Chapter 6

Antero Reservoir

Built to Quench Denver's Thirst

Antero, the sun-sparkled windswept reservoir hidden behind low rolling hills seven miles west of Hartsel, was drained in the spring of 2015 to repair and strengthen the leaking one-hundred-six-year-old dam; water flowed downstream to Cheesman, Marston, and Chatfield reservoirs. It was the eighth time since 1924 that Antero had been drained.

The most recent draining prompted a look back at Antero's 138-year history.

In June 2015, water released from Antero Reservoir mingles with spring runoff from the Buffalo Peaks, resulting in overflow of the South Fork of the South Platte River. *Photo by the author.*

The Beginning

Antero's beginning traces back to 1877, when English capitalists decided to build an irrigation ditch through Denver. They proposed it would transform the surrounding dry prairie into an oasis of trees, flowers, and gardens, and aid farmers and ranchers. The construction contract for that ditch, called the High Line Canal, was signed in November 1879.

The canal made a wonderful improvement to the new city, and hundreds of men were employed to build it. Crops and cattle were healthy, and the city was vibrant with shade and fruit trees and picturesque gardens. Land values boomed with what was thought to be an inexhaustible water supply. As it turned out, there was not enough water for everyone.

Trouble

A short article in the January 16, 1886, *Rocky Mountain News* reported problems with the canal. It seems there were more water applications for the next growing season than could be carried in the ditch. Looking on the bright side, the paper said it was "a good indication of the rapid development" of Denver. It's true the city was growing, but it's also true that water demands for Denver couldn't be met. That was not the only problem. Canal developers learned that people living downstream from Denver relied on that water, and they weren't happy it was taken away.

The High Line was the first canal the South Platte River encountered after passing through Platte Canyon southwest of Denver. Every possible drop of water was diverted into it. In the summer of 1886, ditches that irrigated farmlands northeast of Denver near Greeley, in Weld County, went dry. Those fields had priority water rights over the High Line, yet cattle grazing in the area were dying of thirst; even the native pronghorn were suffering. At the same time, the High Line was reported to be "six feet deep and forty feet wide" running through Denver, according to the July 16, 1886, *Rocky Mountain News.*

And it got worse. In June 1890, the state engineer's office ordered floodgates to Weld County canals closed because, according to the *News* of June 28, water commissioners "find it politic [diplomatic] to side with those people with whom they come most in contact."

A temporary injunction ordered the canal gates open, and angry farmers and ranchers guarded them. They put up signs threatening to kill anyone attempting to close the gates again. Court suits continued for years as details of early Colorado water law were decided.

South Park

It wasn't long before the High Line Canal affected water rights in South Park.

In the summer of 1890, a judge in Colorado Springs ordered twenty-five South Park ditches shut down so that water could flow downriver to the High Line. As a result, in August 1890, the South Park Ranchmen's Protective Association was formed to protect what ranchers believed to be their right to "use as much water as is necessary for irrigating purposes." The irrigated crop was South Park hay, famous throughout the state for its superior quality, according to the *Rocky Mountain News* of August 4, 1890.

Glimmer of Antero

The July 1, 1891, *Rocky Mountain News* said an immense basin—Antero Reservoir—was to be filled with water as a solution to the High Line Canal problems. The paper said Antero—along with Castlewood Reservoir in Douglas County and the proposed Lost Park Reservoir, downstream from Antero—were considered the main water supply for Denver.

(Castlewood Dam, built in 1890, broke in August 1933. The released waters flooded downtown Denver, and the dam was not repaired. The broken dam is now a focal point of Castlewood Canyon State Park near Franktown. Lost Park Reservoir, its former site surrounded by Lost Creek Wilderness in Park County, was a failed attempt to dam Lost Creek. Neither the plan nor the dam held water because, true to the name, the creek was "lost." It flowed underground in the area of the dam.)

According to the *News* story, the site for Antero had been considered several years earlier as a reservoir site. The story said planners at that time met with "a difficulty of securing the funds." Curiously, in the otherwise straightforward story, one sentence was unclear and unexplained. It said, "*Intelligence from the East* [italics added] indicates that work may be commenced before the close of the present season."

Abandoned buildings at the Lost Park Reservoir site. *Photo courtesy of South Park Ranger District, Pike National Forest, Fairplay, Colorado.*

An explanation of "intelligence from the East" could be that the man who owned the Antero site, Peter W. Sheafer, was from the eastern United States. His work as a renowned coal mine engineer, land surveyor, and geologist took him all over the country from his Pottsville, Pennsylvania, base. It can be speculated that Sheafer didn't want to sell the Antero property or that his asking price was considered too high. It could be that when he died in New Jersey on March 26, 1891, the Antero site was reconsidered.

The leader behind the Antero plans in 1891 was Cyrus Greenwood Richardson, a Denver attorney. He owned $1 million worth of land ($26 million in 2015 dollars) with High Line Canal water rights, including the 3,200-acre Greenwood Ranch that is today's upscale Denver suburb Greenwood Village. His plan was to sell water from Antero Reservoir to owners of the High Line.

The first step in building Antero was to acquire the land. In 1892, Richardson put up $10,000 of his own money and attorney Charles H. Burton, who had represented Richardson in another case, began legal condemnation proceedings of the Antero land using Colorado's eminent domain law (the right to take property for a public purpose if the acquisition is necessary for reservoirs, drains, flumes, or ditches for agricultural, mining, milling, domestic, or sanitary purposes). The law provided that the owner be justly compensated for the condemned property.

The estate of Peter W. Sheafer and his heirs—including twenty-five family members, and the Benevolent Association, the Children's Home and the Methodist Episcopal Church, all of Pottsville—settled in November 1892. Their lawyer accepted $18,500 (in 2015 dollars that's $487,000) for them for the tract of land that would become Antero Reservoir.

Richardson's untimely death in 1894 at age fifty-two delayed the plans to build Antero until 1907.

Building the Dam

The Antero project was taken over in April 1907 by several investors, including another wealthy Denver landowner with property along the High Line, Bradford H. DuBois. But he, at least, had interests in South Park.

In 1896, DuBois and Felix Leavick had bought the Hill Top Mine near the town of Leavick, along present-day County Road 18, southwest of Fairplay. Together they built an eleven-mile railroad spur—the Fairplay, South Park and Hilltop—to service the mines along that route. They had also built the mill that, in 2016, still stands on the side of the road near the former Leavick townsite. DuBois had interests in Leadville mines as well; at one time he owned the Chrysolite, and he was one of the discoverers of the Maid of Erin.

In May 1907, Antero project organizers held a meeting with people who owned land along a proposed extension of the High Line between Denver and Greeley. DuBois suggested to the group that a reservoir be built at the Antero site to be owned by all High Line Canal landowners. He said, "with the completion of our new reservoir we will have practically unlimited water supply."

Thirty-three landowners incorporated in October 1907 with capital of $2 million, according to the October 25, 1907, *Flume.* It was called the Antero and Lost Park Reservoir Company, also known as the Antero Company. Their plan was to build two reservoirs—Antero and Lost Park. Contracts were signed in April 1908, with Horace G. Clark appointed as president. Less than a year later, the group bought the High Line Canal, and the name was changed to the Antero Land and Irrigation Company. It was still called the Antero Company.

That summer, several hundred men were hard at work in South Park. A headline in the *Flume* of August 7, 1908, said the "Great Antero Dam" would soon begin storing water. By June 1909, the water was nine feet deep.

A summer day at Antero Reservoir, September 2013. *Photo by the author.*

Litigation

Ranchers in South Park could watch only so long as less water flowed down the South Platte and into the ditches they had used since the 1860s. In the summer of 1910, the South Park Ranchmen's Protective Association brought suit in Denver District Court, accusing the Antero Company of "impounding water contrary to law," according to the July 15, 1910, *Flume*. The ranchmen said that four and a half times more water came into Antero than was released below the dam. The reservoir company filed a counterclaim against the ranchers, saying they were taking water that they had no right to take.

They were both right. The Antero Company, when reporting the amount of water that flowed into the reservoir, counted only water coming in from the main channel of the South Platte River, not the numerous small streams and springs that also fed Antero. And the South Park ranchers were guilty because they didn't close their headgates when ordered to do so by the state water commissioner. Even when the headgates were closed, they were set so high that plenty of water flowed underneath to provide irrigation.

The essence of the two suits concerned priority water rights. Colorado water law, then and now, gives priority, or first, water rights to the party who is first to physically take water from a stream or aquifer for a beneficial use. The priority has to be by court decree, or adjudication, verifying who has priority status. If two or more parties have senior rights, then domestic use is given priority over agricultural use.

The judge ruled in favor of the reservoir company and ordered all South Park ranchers to be restricted from opening the headgates to their ditches to capture either the direct flow of the river or water released from the reservoir. The division engineer and water commissioner from Denver were in South Park the day after the ruling to close down all headgates on the Middle and South Forks of the South Platte south and east of Fairplay; they hired guards to enforce compliance.

In May 1911, another judge ruled that the same amount of water that flowed into the reservoir should also flow out of Antero; simultaneously, the water commissioner closed all South Park ditches with priority dates later than May 6, 1866, which blocked all but two South Park ditches.

A celebration was held in June 1913 in fields northeast of Denver when the High Line Canal Extension was opened. Thousands of people witnessed Governor Elias Ammons christen the "great Antero system" that was expected to "turn 60,000 acres of barren land into green, productive fields," according to the June 27, 1913, *Routt County Republican.*

Three years later, the Antero Company had oversold again. It couldn't provide enough water for sugar beet fields near Greeley. Antero Company President Clark told farmers to blame "the lawless ditch owners of South Park" for stealing water, according to a letter by Clark printed in the June 16, 1916, *Record-Journal of Douglas County* and reprinted on July 7 in the *Flume.*

Clark also attributed the lack of water to the engineering firm hired to dig the extension, Henry L. Doherty and Company, accusing it of failing to build the system according to specifications. When the promised water couldn't be supplied through the extension, Clark refused to pay Doherty. The real reason for nonpayment, historians have speculated, was that negotiations were in process for sale of the system to Denver.

The High Line Canal north of Montview Boulevard, east of downtown Denver, in 1941. *Photo courtesy of Denver Water, March 23, 2015.*

Sale to Denver

In 1915, the population of Denver was nearing a quarter of a million people. By 1920, it was the twenty-fifth most populous city in the nation, and its citizens needed more water. On August 21, 1915, the Public Utilities Commission of Denver made an offer to buy Antero Reservoir and the High Line Canal for its municipal water system.

Almost as soon as the contract was announced, an injunction was filed by Doherty to prevent the sale until his company was paid for the High Line Extension work. The litigation, and other suits related to the failure of the canal to supply water to farmers' fields, lasted for five years. The suits were settled in the Antero Company's favor in November 1920. Denver Water, which took over as water supplier for the city in 1918, finalized the contract with the Antero Company and has owned both Antero Reservoir and the High Line Canal since 1924.

Today

Antero, along with three other reservoirs (Spinney Mountain, Eleven Mile, and Montgomery) and a natural lake (Jefferson), provide South Park water to Front Range cities. Their impact on the ranching industry is huge.

In 1930, South Park supported up to 394 ranches in a vast sea of grassy meadows. By 1950, only 120 working ranches remained. In 2015, nineteen ranches in South Park retained full pre-1900 water rights, and about six more retained a portion of original water rights or had acquired other senior water rights. Only six of those operated as year-round ranches, according to Garver Brown, Division 1 water commissioner with the Colorado Division of Water Resources.

Antero Reservoir has a decreed capacity of eighty-five thousand acre-feet, equal to a thirty-six-foot depth at the Antero site (an acre foot is the amount of water it takes to cover one acre of land to a depth of one foot). However, since the 1930s, state engineers have limited the capacity of Antero to twenty thousand acre-feet or less (equal to an eighteen-foot depth) due to the dam's dirt construction. The new 2015 Antero dam will bear a depth of twenty-six feet; Denver Water plans to hold Antero to an eighteen-foot depth for the foreseeable future, according to documents on its website.

The High Line Canal, a designated National Landmark Trail, has extremely limited irrigation use today. It is a sixty-six-mile-long scenic recreational trail, winding through Douglas, Arapahoe, and Denver Counties from Waterton Canyon (near Wadsworth Boulevard and C-470) to the Green Valley Ranch subdivision (near Tower Road and East 56th Avenue).

Why Drained

According to Jeremy Allen with Denver Water, the reservoir was lowered by about one foot in 1958 to comply with a dam restriction. In 1986, and again in 1996, Antero was drained for maintenance work on the outlet structure. In drought years, the reservoir is drained and the water moved downstream to deeper reservoirs to minimize evaporation. That was the reason for the drains in 1925, 1931, 1951, 1963, and 2002. In future drought years, Antero will likely be emptied again.

1880s

Chapter 7

Como: The First Six Years

Rowdy, Coal-Mining Railroad Hub

In January 2015, there were seventeen full-time residents and only one permanent business in the town of Como. In contrast, the month-old Como, in July 1879, saw bustling streets, train arrivals and departures at all hours, and a flourishing business community.

In its early years, Como attracted a rowdy international crowd of railroad workers, gold miners, and coal diggers. Not everyone got along. Through 1885, gunfire was common—four men were murdered in those first six years; a fifth killing was ruled self-defense.

Coal mine superintendent Edward L. Thayer was severely beaten during an employment dispute brought on by Italian miners in November 1879. Called the "Como War," it happened only five months after the first tents were pitched at the new end-of-the-line railroad town. Thayer was lucky to survive.

It's no wonder the *Fairplay Flume* of November 10, 1881, said, "The state of society now existing at Como is about as bad as can be imagined."

Still, the town thrived.

A large school was built on a hill above town, and churches of several denominations held weekly services. Dances sponsored by the Como Social Club were held every other Friday evening alternately at the school house, the Como and Gilman Hotels, and the town hall.

Como was the most populated town in the county in the early years, and talk in 1884 proposed moving the county seat to Como from Fairplay. Buildings still standing in Como today date from those first years, including the depot, the roundhouse, the elementary school, the Catholic church, and the Montag Saloon.

Historical restoration of the Como Depot was completed on October 8, 2014, prompting a look back at Como's early years.

Como, Colorado, in 1883. *George Mellen photo, courtesy of the Bill Eloe Collection, sepia tone removed, cropped.*

Como Start

The town had its start in June 1879, when rails for the Denver, South Park & Pacific narrow-gauge railroad topped Kenosha Pass. Tracks were laid to Jefferson and continued another five miles to a flat meadow near the foot of Little Baldy Mountain. The town that grew there was named Como.

The name Como was already being used by another settlement, about three miles to the southeast near the lower mines of the South Park Coal Company. However, the name "Como" stuck with the end-of-track settlement. It was the more important of the two Como's and grew to become the division point for Denver trains traveling northwest over Boreas Pass to Breckenridge, south to Nathrop, and west through the Alpine Tunnel to Gunnison.

The town near the lower mines was renamed King, also called King City and King Park.

Magic City

A story in the July 17, 1879, *Flume* describes the "Magic City of Como that has risen in thirty days." It called Como "the liveliest town of its size in the state." There were sixty or seventy tents used both as residences and businesses, and up to a dozen wooden structures.

A TENTED TOWN.

THE MAGIC CITY OF COMO THAT HAS RISEN IN THIRTY DAYS.

Headline in the July, 17, 1879, *Fairplay Flume. Clip courtesy of Colorado Historic Newspapers, www.ColoradoHistoricNewspapers.org.*

The main business was the railroad. Twenty carloads of freight arrived from Denver daily, and with the activity of loading and unloading, it was undoubtedly noisy. Trains returning to Denver hauled gold and other precious minerals from the mines in Fairplay, Alma, and Breckenridge; coal from Como and King; and ice cut from Lake Como. In the first month of its existence, passenger travel between Denver and Como was considered heavy, with up to twenty people per day traveling north to Denver, and many times that number traveling south to Como.

The *Flume* reported the entire town of Como was built on a "magnificent vein of coal" up to eight feet thick. The paper predicted that by the following winter the coal mines would employ one hundred men and produce three hundred tons of coal per day.

Early Businesses

Within a month of its founding, business was booming in Como.

Three freighting companies were in operation. They transported goods on wagons and sold groceries, clothing, and general merchandise on the side. One freighter dealt in fresh fruits and vegetables, probably a welcome commodity in the high-elevation mountain town.

Narrow-gauge train on Boreas Pass, between Como and Breckenridge, late 1800s. *Park County Local History Archives, South Park Historical Foundation.*

Ed's Restaurant, the O.K. Restaurant, the South Park Railroad Eating House, and A.C. Edwards' Dining Hall welcomed customers with meals any time of the day or night. In a tent above the permanent wooden structure of Ed's Restaurant was Hamilton's Barber Shop.

In its first years, Como had a meat market, a combination livery stable and lumberyard, a harness shop, clothing and general merchandise stores, one bakery, two stage lines, a billiard hall, a few hotels, and at least six saloons. Some saloons had a relaxed atmosphere, like the Club House, billed as "a place to spend a quiet hour and enjoy a glass of Milwaukee or Budweiser beer," and the Gold Room, "a neat and orderly house." Others attracted a more boisterous crowd.

One saloon described at length in the July 17, 1879, *Flume*, was Dodge's Footlights and Varieties. It claimed order was kept and police were not necessary. The *Flume* called it free and easy, a fun-for-all place typical of a frontier town.

Dodge's consisted of a pavilion, thirty-three feet by eighty feet, with an attached eighteen-foot by thirty-foot tent and a bar that measured twenty-five feet long. The dance floor took up half the tent, where "many hundreds congregate every night." They danced to lively piano music accompanied by strumming guitars and vocals of the house band.

Games of chance were played in the saloon, including high ball poker, roulette, twenty-one, faro, and chuck-a-luck (played with three dice).

The former Montag Saloon, later called the Diamond Bar, Como, Colorado, September 2012. *Photo by the author.*

Murder at the Montag

The Montag Saloon was another early drinking establishment. The building has been vacant for years but is still standing on the corner of Sixth and Rowe Streets. On September 26, 1881, it was the scene of one of the town's first murders. The *Flume* of September 29, 1881, said that James Donley (or Donneli) and John Lyons were both at the saloon when one of Donley's friends hit Lyons. Lyons told the man not to do that again and then left the saloon.

Lyons returned a short time later and encountered Donley. A fight broke out between the two, and they "grappled and rolled together on the floor." Soon it was a free-for-all as several other men joined in the fight, "rolling on the floor together," according to the *Flume* story. During the fight, Lyons pulled out his revolver, fired it, and hit Donley. At first, nobody believed the shot would prove fatal, according to the *Flume*. Donley was taken to a Denver hospital on the train, and Lyons was jailed in Fairplay. But Donley died soon after, apparently from the gunshot, although Lyons said the victim had a "foul disease, which caused death as much as his wound."

Before his trial, Lyons was held at the Park County jail in Fairplay, where another man, Fred Dier, attempted unsuccessfully to help Lyons escape. At trial, the jury could not decide on a verdict, and Lyons was returned to jail. Dier was also held. In June 1882, both Lyons and Dier were shackled together with ball and chain doing yard work on the courthouse lawn. There was no guard present, and it appeared the two "had provided themselves with a key" to unlock the anklet, according to the *Flume* of June 29, 1882. They escaped into a thicket of underbrush and were not seen or heard from again.

Deadly Argument

The very first recorded death by gunshot in Como happened in December 1879, according to the December 11 and 12, 1879, editions of the *Rocky Mountain News.*

J. W. Laughlin and Augustus (Gus) Cornog were guards for the South Park Coal Company and shared a company cabin. On the evening of December 9, 1879, Laughlin was inside the cabin when Cornog came in and dumped kerosene on the fire to help it burn. In the process, he spilled some of the oil on Laughlin.

Laughlin told Cornog to be careful. The two argued. Cornog pulled out a revolver as if to shoot Laughlin, but he didn't shoot. Laughlin picked up his Winchester rifle, telling Cornog he shouldn't pull a gun on an unarmed man. Then Cornog again pointed his revolver and made a move as if to shoot. Laughlin fired the rifle at Cornog, who died almost instantly. Laughlin pled self-defense at his trial in November 1880 and was acquitted.

Como War

Both Laughlin and Cornog were guards hired to keep the peace after the "Como War," a confrontation described in the November 13, 1879, *Fairplay Flume.*

It all started on Sunday, November 9, when Italians working the coal mines near the railroad tracks at Como became upset when two of their race were fired and replaced by Chinese workers. A group of thirty Italians approached the Chinese and told them to leave the country at once, threatening to cut off their queues "three inches south of their ears" if they didn't leave.

(Queue refers to a traditional Manchu, or northeastern China, hairstyle in which the front and sides of the head are shaved and the rest of the hair is plaited into a long braid. Since 1644, when the Manchu conquered China, all Chinese men were required to wear a queue hairstyle. It was an act of treason punishable by beheading to cut the queue. Because most Chinese men working in nineteenth-century America planned to return to China within a few years, they wanted to keep their queues.)

When the Chinese didn't leave by the following Tuesday, the Italians tried to convince mine superintendent Edward L. Thayer to fire the Chinese. They surrounded him as he walked to the Como Depot. Thayer calmly greeted the miners but refused their request. The Italians became angry, so Thayer authoritatively pulled out his revolver. That caused all the Italians to ready their guns; they told Thayer to drop his weapon, and he did.

The Italians countered Thayer's refusal by throwing him to the ground. They stomped on him and pounded him with the butts of their rifles. Thayer was at a double disadvantage: one, he was outnumbered, and, two, he had only one arm; his right arm had been amputated years before. The crowd became more violent. A pistol barrel was placed at the back of Thayer's head and fired at close range. Luckily for Thayer, he was also hit or shoved by one of the Italians at the same time. When the gun discharged, the bullet glanced off his skull and gave him a "severe concussion, but no wound to speak of," the *Flume* story said.

The thirty Italians who started the turmoil were fired, and Italians and Chinese, along with other nationalities, continued to work the mines together, until at least 1885. The *Flume* of May 28, 1885, said all the Chinese miners had left.

Good Times

It wasn't all bad news in Como's first years. The Fourth of July was celebrated in style.

A rousing fifty-five-gun salute followed by fireworks woke Como residents on July 4, 1882. Then a "procession of comical vagabonds" led celebrants to the town picnic grounds, where Judge Webster Ballinger read the Declaration of Independence before the beginning of the games: foot races, horse races, and contests of athletic ability. The games were followed by a grand ball in the evening, sponsored by the Union Circle of United Irishmen of Como.

Three years later, the Independence Day celebration began with a parade. The Como Cornet Band and Select Knights of the Ancient Order of United Workmen (AOUW)—a fraternal organization similar to the Masons—led the way. Afternoon activities included foot races and a baseball game. A dance was held Friday, July 3, at the Gilman Hotel, and another was held July 4 at the town hall.

A cornet band, similar to this one from early-1900s Como, led the Fourth of July parade in 1885. *Park County Local History Archives.*

Como also had cultured entertainment. In early 1885, a group called the Como Colored Concert Coterie put on a minstrel show in the town hall, followed by a burlesque called *The Black Justice*. A few weeks later, the Como Dramatic Club brought in a national entertainer, comedian Harry Webber. His troupe, with wife Eva and six-year-old daughter Carrie, was popular in the East.

The troupe played in Aspen and Denver before a two-night Como engagement in late May 1885, where they performed *Blunders*, *Bessie's Burglar*, and *Nip and Tuck*.

Maturing

After the turbulent first six years, Como gradually adopted a gentler attitude. Only two murders made the news in the next fifteen years. Railroad workers brought their families to Como, and interest turned to schools, baseball games, fishing, and politics. Contributing to the calm was the closing of the coal mines in the early 1900s and the end-of-the-track tent city moving on down the line.

Chapter 8

Edward L. Thayer

"Captain Sam"

In November 1879, Edward L. Thayer was the employment superintendent for coal mines at Como and King. He was attacked and nearly killed by Italian miners in the Como War when he refused to fire Chinese workers.

THE COMO WAR.

Full Particulars of the assult upon Mr. E. L. Thayer,

Headline in the *Fairplay Flume* of November 13, 1879. *Clip courtesy of Colorado Historic Newspapers, www.ColoradoHistoricNewspapers.org.*

Thayer was born in 1831, the son of a wealthy high-society Boston family. He left home at age eighteen to find his own fortune in the 1849 California Gold Rush and died penniless in 1893 in Denver's Arapahoe County Hospital. (The hospital was later called Denver General Hospital and is, in 2016, Denver Health Medical Center. Denver County, not yet established in 1893, was formed in 1902 from a small portion of Arapahoe County.)

Placer mining in 1849 California was lucrative for Thayer; he made "quite a fortune out of the dust," said his obituary in the June 4, 1893, *Rocky Mountain News*. The gold rush attracted people from all over the world, including many from China. It was probably there that Thayer met Chinese immigrants for the first time. Thayer later became a Chinese employment contractor, helping Chinese immigrants find jobs in the United States. In 1863 and 1864, he worked for the Central Pacific Railroad, supplying and supervising Chinese workers as they helped build the California-to-Utah portion of the Transcontinental Railroad.

Thayer learned the Chinese language and lifestyle both in his work in the States and in a visit to China in 1873. He was respected by the Chinese workers. They regarded him as a friend and trusted counselor, and they called him "Captain Sam."

On November 30, 1874, Thayer and business partner Lewis Dibble opened a shop selling Chinese and Japanese merchandise at 402 Larimer Street in Denver—part of the Auraria Campus complex in 2016. They sold colorful kites, fans, and lanterns; high-quality items made of wood, ivory, and gold; and imported teas and sugars. In the mid-1870s, Thayer came to Fairplay, where he was responsible for hiring four hundred Chinese workers for the Platte Gulch placer mines there.

In 1879, he began working for the South Park Coal Mines at Como and King, supervising one hundred workers, about half of them Chinese. According to his obituary in the June 8, 1893, *Flume*, Thayer was almost penniless when he started working in Como and King. The *Flume* said his poverty was due to "disasters in mining," which possibly meant unsuccessful mining ventures. He was an amputee by 1879, but no public record could be found regarding when and where it happened. The only mention found was in the *Flume*'s November 13, 1879, story about the Como War, which referred to "his right arm having long since suffered amputation above the elbow."

When he wasn't working, Thayer was involved with the Park County Republicans and was asked by the party to be their candidate for sheriff in 1885. Thayer declined because, according to the September 24, 1885, *Flume*, he didn't think he would win due to his previous association with the Chinese (who were held in low esteem).

A January 1890 snowstorm was the beginning of Thayer's downfall. He traveled between Como and Fairplay during the storm, and upon arrival in

Fairplay became paralyzed on his left side, possibly due to a stroke. He hoped to find a cure, and, using his savings and help from friends, he went to a hospital in Tewksbury, Massachusetts. Available records don't indicate why Thayer chose Tewksbury. The hospital, established in 1854 and still operational in 2016, is twenty-four miles northeast of Boston. In 1879, it was not known for treating stroke patients; it specialized in treating indigent patients with infectious diseases and the mentally ill. Maybe Thayer chose it because it was close to his childhood home.

The *Flume* obituary reported that, although he partially recovered from the paralysis, "from that time he was never himself again."

The disabled and completely broke Thayer returned to Colorado, and was taken in by one of his former employees, Chin Poo, the manager of a Chinese/Japanese merchandise store. He lived in a shanty near 16th and Wazee Streets, then in the heart of Denver's Chinatown.

In 1892, Thayer developed gangrene in his feet, and it spread throughout his body. He was admitted to the Arapahoe County Hospital for treatment three times within two years. The last time he didn't survive.

Edward L. Thayer, age sixty-two, died on Saturday, June 3, 1893. His obituary in the June 4, 1893, *Rocky Mountain News*, said he would be buried "as soon as his friends can meet to raise the funds." His burial site is unknown.

1890s

Chapter 9

Lewis Martin Link

Clips from a Colorful Life

When twenty-one-year-old Elizabeth Whitley Martin Link cradled her firstborn for the first time, she must have wondered—as most new mothers do—what he would become. She probably hoped he would lead a good life and make his parents proud. And if she could have seen into the future, she surely would have wished she could have shielded him from some of the heartache and violence he would experience in his short fifty-six years.

Lewis Martin Link was born in 1845 in St. Louis, Missouri, to James M. and Elizabeth Link. Of the eight siblings, only two lived a long life; sister Nancy died at age eighty-one, and brother Celsus was seventy at his death. Lew, as he was commonly called, never knew that his brother William was to die of heart problems in 1912 at age fifty-two or that his brother James would be murdered in Guatemala in 1913 at age fifty-seven.

Lew also never knew that, in a crime of passion, his son Truman Link was to shoot and kill first cousin Ned Link (a son of James) in 1907. He couldn't have known, because those events happened after Lew's stabbing death in 1901 at a Castle Dale, Utah, saloon.

The Link family figured prominently in Park County history in the late 1800s. Lew was an Alma marshal and saloon owner, William served at separate times as county assessor and county treasurer, and Celsus was at different times Fairplay mayor, deputy county treasurer, county assessor, and Colorado tax commissioner. Their brother James was the Park County deputy sheriff who arrested both Levi Streeter—for the murder of Como Marshal Adolph Cook in 1894—and Benjamin Ratcliff, who killed three Michigan Creek school board members near Jefferson in 1895.

Lew's portrait was taken in about 1895, when he was fifty years old. The photocopy of that portrait is of too poor resolution to be reproduced for this book, but it shows him as a slender white man with a thick moustache and full head of hair cut in a fashionably short style. He is dressed in a suit and tie.

He made the news frequently in his lifetime, as a marshal and saloon keeper in Alma, as a defendant in a charge of assault and battery upon the *Flume* publisher in 1897, and as the owner of a Salt Lake City saloon where two black men were shot in 1900. His life-ending, possibly unprovoked, stabbing at the Court Saloon was covered extensively by Utah newspapers.

The Beginning

During the Civil War, Missouri was a border state; soldiers were recruited for both sides, its state star was on both flags, and it had separate governments representing the Confederacy and the Union. In 1861, Lew, at age sixteen, joined the Confederate Army with his father, according to a lengthy obituary in the August 24, 1901, *Emery County (Utah) Progress.*

In 1867, he and Virginia Shuwalter married. The June 1870 census recorded the young couple and five-month-old Truman living in Missouri with Lew's parents and siblings. In 1872, the family was living in Alma, Colorado, where their second child and first daughter, Elizabeth—called Bessie—was born. Three years later, on March 4, 1875, the couple's third child, Eleanor, was born. She died on Valentine's Day in 1878, two weeks before her third birthday. Eleanor is buried at Alma's Buckskin Cemetery—the only Link family member buried there.

Lew Link had success locating the Truman Lode in Mosquito Gulch in July 1878. Probably named after his son, it yielded gray copper, an ore frequently interspersed with silver. Soon after the discovery, an assay showed 3,410 ounces of silver to the ton, or "a coin value of over $3,700 per ton," according to the July 3, 1879, *Flume.* Converted to 2015 dollars, the assay showed a worth of $88,000 per ton.

But wealth was not in the cards for Link. He lost his one-half interest in a sheriff's sale on October 23, 1880, to settle a $572.14 debt (about $13,300 in 2015 dollars).

The J. J. Neary Pool Room in the 1890s, near Main and Buckskin Streets in Alma, Colorado. In the 1870s, Lew Link owned the Corner Saloon on this site. *Photo from the personal collection of Erik C. Swanson.*

Marshal Link

When Link was marshal of Alma in 1879 and 1880, it was a rowdy frontier town in the midst of its second silver boom (between 1878, when bimetallism was partially restored, and 1893, when the Sherman Silver Purchase Act was repealed). Everybody, it seemed, carried a gun, and shootings were common.

On the evening of March 22, 1880, Link was on duty when Irish miner Thomas Carmody, age twenty-nine, joined patrons in an area bar where the conversation turned to religion. After the discussion, the group dispersed and Carmody encountered forty-two-year-old William Porter on the street. Porter had been involved in the discussion in the saloon and indicated then that he didn't like Carmody's viewpoint. After more shouting, he shot Carmody in the chest point-blank and without warning.

Even though the wound would soon prove fatal, Carmody ran away. Porter prepared to take another shot when Marshal Link knocked him cold with the cane he always carried. Porter didn't regain consciousness until after he was incarcerated in the Alma jail.

"Excitement was at a fever heat throughout the town," the March 25, 1880, *Flume*, reported. "Never before has Park County witnessed a more unjustifiable, more unprovoked and cold-blooded murder."

Apparently Alma townspeople thought so too.

"Nearly every able-bodied man in the town had assembled on Main Street and excited cries of 'Hang the murderer!' were heard," said the *Flume*.

It was one hour after Carmody had been shot—and only thirty minutes after he had died—that residents convinced Marshal Link to hand over the keys to the jail so they wouldn't have to break down the door to get at Porter. Link at first refused but later realized it was useless to fight the whole town and gave up the keys. Soon after that, townspeople lynched Porter from the ridgepole of the jail's roof. The local coroner's jury (a group summoned to assist a coroner in determining the cause of death) determined Porter died by hanging "at the hands of persons to the jury unknown."

"Persons to the jury unknown" was probably a stretch; it was likely at least some of the jury members were part of the lynch mob or knew who was, but frontier justice prevailed, and no further legal action was taken.

The citizens of Alma didn't hold Link responsible for the lynching; in fact, they honored him for his handling of the situation. A citizens' committee endorsed "his prompt and fearless action." They exonerated him from "all blame in giving up the keys of the jail which he did under a pressure that no man could resist," read the resolution of the citizens' committee, as reported in the March 25, 1880, *Flume*.

Residents of Alma donated liberally to a fund, and Lew M. Link was presented with a gold masonic badge and a .41-caliber Colt revolver, described as a silver-mounted, pearl-handled, double-action piece. An inscription on the handle read: "Presented to L. M. Link by the citizens of Alma, for his prompt and fearless performance of duty on March 22nd, 1880."

The gun was in Link's hand when he died.

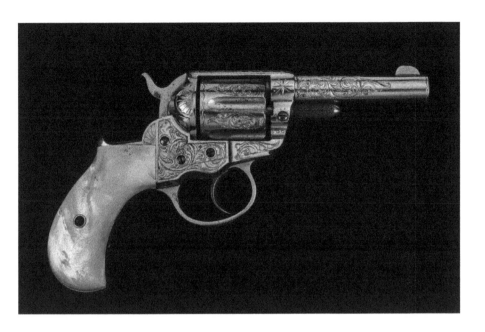

The .41-caliber silver-mounted, pearl-handled, double-action Colt revolver presented to Lew Link could be one of only two models, according to Colt expert, antique gun dealer, and Old West historian Kurt House of Old West Collectibles in San Antonio, Texas. It was either the 1877 model shown above or the 1878 model shown below. The photos are from his file. *Kurt House Collection, Paul Goodwin, photographer. Photos used with permission.*

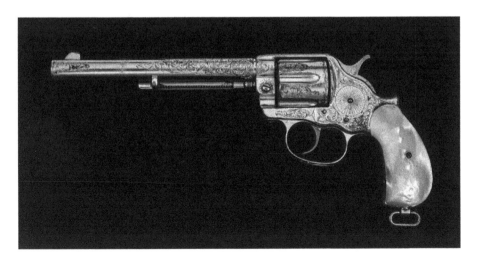

Flume Publisher Attacked

Lew, his brother Celsus, and town attorney Augustus (Gus) Pease learned a lesson from the *Flume* publisher in October 1897—don't get on the bad side of the power of the pen.

A one-sided story printed in the October 22, 1897, *Flume*, told readers that William Link, Park County treasurer, drew $787 more in salary per year than he was entitled and that he hired his brother Celsus Link as deputy treasurer, paying him $900 per year. The story said that previous treasurers had hired clerks when help was needed and that they had never hired a full-time assistant. The publisher, George Miller, also accused William Link of other unethical, if not illegal, bookkeeping practices during his years in office.

A week later, Lew and Celsus Link and town attorney Pease walked into the *Flume* office. According to publisher Miller, Celsus struck him repeatedly while the other two guarded the room to prevent interference. Miller claimed the trio's plan was to print their own version of the next edition, including a retraction of the October 22 story.

Citizens, hearing Miller's cries as he was allegedly hit by Celsus, rushed to the newspaper office to stop the beating and the printing of the altered edition. The three went to court in the last week of November 1897. Celsus Link and Gus Pease were each fined $25 (about $700 in 2015 dollars). Lew Link was fined $5 (about $140 in 2015 dollars), and all three were lectured by Judge John Ifinger.

Following the incident, William Link lost his November 2, 1897, re-election bid for treasurer and did not hold public office again. Celsus Link later served as mayor of Fairplay, district court clerk, county assessor, and Colorado state tax assessor. He earned the right to choose stories for the *Flume* as its owner and publisher from 1906 to 1912. Also in 1912, attorney Pease was appointed a district court judge.

As for Lew Link, in 1898 he went to Utah.

Salt Lake City

Public records were not available to show when Lew Link and his wife, Virginia, separated, but she did not make the move to Utah. She, along with their daughter Bessie, was living in Colorado Springs in 1900. Son Truman's trail was lost until August 1907, when he made the news in El Paso, Texas.

In Salt Lake City, Lew owned Link's Saloon at State and Second South Streets, near the Fort Douglas army base. Being so close to the base, business was good, especially on paydays. Link, however, tried to discourage some soldiers from drinking at his establishment. He posted a sign at the bar saying, "All drinks served here to colored people 25¢." That was five times the amount charged for white customers.

The sign "aroused the ire of the colored people . . . who had been in the habit of quenching their thirst at that place," said a story in the May 15, 1900, *Salt Lake Tribune*.

At first, black soldiers avoided Link's Saloon but, the *Tribune* reported, "an agitator amongst them (said that) any man, no matter what his color, had a right to drink beer if he had the coin . . . to pay for it, irrespective of his color." The agitator also proposed all customers should pay the same price.

The difference in beliefs came to a head on May 14, 1900. Shortly after 9 p.m., five black men came into the saloon. Bartender Fred Maddick pointed out the twenty-five cent cost of drinks, and the group agreed to the price. But when the soldiers left, they paid twenty-five cents for the whole bill, not for each drink, which angered Maddick. As they walked out, the bartender handed a gun to his son, Will Maddick, who was standing by the door, and asked Will to stop them.

Apparently, rocks were thrown at the younger Maddick, but he thought it was a bullet that hit his head. In retaliation, he shot into the crowded street and hit two black men, one of whom was not even in the bar earlier. Both were seriously injured and had long recovery periods, and both survived. Maddick was acquitted by the court for one shooting; no reason for the acquittal was given in newspaper reports. Charges were dismissed in the other case because the soldier was serving in the Philippines at the time and was unavailable to testify.

Castle Dale

Two months later, Link left Salt Lake City and moved to Kaysville, twenty miles north. He opened a saloon there with Will Maddick as his employee. It was a quiet ten months at the Kaysville saloon, at least according to available public records. Link may have been restless, or perhaps business wasn't so good. He moved again in the spring of 1901, this time to the canyon country of Castle Dale, Utah, 170 miles south of Kaysville. It was his final move.

At the turn of the twentieth century, Castle Dale had a population of 559. Two saloons served the residents, the Dale Saloon and Link's establishment, the Court Saloon, so named because it was near the courthouse. He lost his life in his saloon in a dispute with two brothers on Saturday, August 17, 1901, minutes before the typical midnight closing.

Undated photo of the Court Saloon, Castle Dale, Utah. *Courtesy of Emery County (Utah) Archives.*

Stories of the stabbing appeared in papers all over Utah, all with slightly different versions. The *Emery County Progress* got it factually right (if not grammatically correct) when it said, "No two witnesses can hardly tell the same story of the killing." Nor did the newspapers tell it quite the same. Combining stories from several sources, the following version may be closest to the truth:

Fred Mickel (or Mickle) was age twenty-seven and single; his brother Pete Mickel was age thirty, married, and the father of two daughters. The brothers were sheep ranchers, born and raised in Utah's canyon country. Newspaper stories of the day said the two were part of the Wild Bunch gang who frequented the Robber's Roost hideout near today's Canyonlands National Park. At the time, Pete was out on bail, pending appeal from a charge of horse theft.

The two had been drinking heavily on the day of the stabbing and had arrived at Link's saloon an hour before midnight. Link was playing cards with some customers, a violinist was playing in the background, and Ed Fox was tending bar. Marshal Samuel Acord was outside the door, waiting for the midnight hour, when he could witness the saloon closing on time.

The Mickel brothers wanted to join in the card game, but Link told them to play at another table. That angered Fred, who tipped the table, making cards and poker chips scatter. Link and Pete Mickel quarreled, with Pete calling Link a "lowdown Southerner" and a "damned Rebel," among other things. Link returned insults of his own. Fred Mickel remained silent.

Those present in the saloon broke up the row and suggested they all have a drink to clear the air. Link agreed and was in the process of filling glasses when Fred Mickel threw a heavy beer glass and hit Link in the face. By then Link knew trouble was brewing. He made his way to the end of the bar, where he kept his gun (the pearl-handled Colt presented by Alma residents in 1880). He grabbed the gun at about the same time Fred Mickel buried the thin, sharp, three-and-one-half-inch blade of a new pocketknife into Link's chest.

In the confusion that followed, both Mickels were handcuffed and subdued. Then attention was directed at Link, lying in a pool of blood behind the bar, deceased.

The family in Park County was notified, and William Link arrived in time to attend the funeral, presided over by Orange Seely, bishop in The Church of Jesus Christ of Latter-Day Saints (Mormon). Plans were for William to escort the remains back to Fairplay for burial, but it was later decided to bury Lew Link at Castle Dale City Cemetery.

Court Ruling

"Lew M. Link Foully Assassinated by Fred Mickel Saturday Night," read the headline of the August 24, 1901, *Emery County Progress.*

MURDER AT CASTLEDALE.

Lew M. Link Foully Assassinated by Fred Mickel Saturday Night.

Headline in the August 24, 1901, *Emery County (Utah) Progress. Clip courtesy of Utah Historic Newspapers, www.digitalnewspapers.org.*

Salt Lake City's *Deseret Evening News* of August 19, 1901, said, "Murder Committed in a Saloon at Castle Dale."

And Price's August 22, 1901, *Eastern Utah Advocate,* said, "Lew M. Link Murdered."

If newspapers decided guilt, it probably would have ended differently for the Mickel brothers. But there was a change in venue to Manti, Utah, twenty-two miles from the Mickels' hometown of Spring City. The trial was held in January 1902, and, in "rather a surprise," Marshal Acord, who was called as a witnesses for the prosecution, gave testimony that favored the defense, said the January 23, 1902, *Ephraim (Utah) Enterprise.*

According to the *Enterprise,* Marshal Acord testified that before Link was stabbed, Acord heard Pete Mickel say, "Mr. Link, put down that gun; I don't want any trouble. I can't afford to have trouble."

Fred Mickel testified in his own defense and said he was the only one who had a full view of Link behind the bar before the stabbing. Fred said Link had the gun in his hand ready to shoot, and that he (Fred) stabbed Link to save Pete. The jury deliberated for an hour and found Fred Mickel not guilty.

Link Family Fate

Misfortune followed other members of the Link family in the first two decades of the twentieth century:

William Link

According to his obituary in the January 3, 1913, *Flume*, Lew's brother William died suddenly of heart trouble in December 1912 in Breckenridge, Colorado. The snow was deep in the high country that winter, which delayed plans for William's funeral and burial. His remains were temporarily interred in Breckenridge until crews working from both sides of Boreas Pass cleared the route. William was later buried in the family plot at Como Cemetery.

James A. Link

Before finding work as a train conductor in Guatemala in January 1913, Lew's brother James had worked trains in Mexico for about ten years. On February 11, 1913, a noisy, drunk passenger threatened other passengers with a gun. James took the gun away, and went to the next car. When James returned to the car, he was fatally stabbed in the lungs by the same drunk passenger. James was buried at Guatemala City Cemetery. The family had plans to bring the body back to the Como Cemetery, but it is unknown if that happened. There is no marker for him there.

Truman, Sarita, and Ned Link

On August 2, 1907, Lew's only son, Truman Curtis Link, thirty-seven, returned to his home in El Paso, Texas, after a four-month absence in Mexico. He had planned to take his wife, Sarita, and their three-year-old son to Mexico, where Truman was employed. When he arrived, his wife was sitting in a chair on the porch, and Truman's cousin Edward "Ned" Link, twenty-three, was in a hammock playing with Truman's son, also named Truman.

When he saw Ned on the porch, Truman took out a revolver. With a single shot he killed Ned, luckily missing little Truman. With another shot, he wounded Sarita; that shot was not fatal, and Truman claimed it was an accident. Truman Link accused his cousin and Sarita of having "improper relations" and said he had warned the two to stay away from each other.

Truman was arrested, posted bail, and, within a few days, had returned to Mexico. A funeral was held for Ned Link on August 5, 1907, in El Paso. He is buried at that city's Concordia Cemetery in a plot reserved for members of the Brotherhood of Locomotive Firemen.

On August 12, 1907, Sarita filed for divorce, saying Truman was "guilty of excesses, cruel treatment and outrages of such a nature that further living together would be unbearable," according to the August 13, 1907, *El Paso Daily Times*. Following the divorce petition, the trail of Sarita and the child faded.

Truman later married Beatrice Cole. They were living in Mazatlán, Mexico, in April 1911 when their son, Howard Rico (or Ricer) Link, was born.

Truman Link died in Del Norte County, California, in March 1930 at age sixty-two. He is buried at the Crescent City Cemetery there.

The Mickels

Pete Mickel lived to age fifty; Fred Mickel was eighty-two when he died. They are both buried in Utah's Spring City Cemetery.

Chapter 10

Disaster at the King Coal Mine

Twenty-Four Dead in the Blink of an Eye

January is typically considered a month of new beginnings, a clean slate to be filled with future hopes and dreams. But in 1893, the New Year brought devastation and sorrow for the residents of King City, a small company town three miles southeast of Como.

King City—also called King and King Park—had a population of three hundred in 1893; two hundred were men employed in the coal mines a mile or so north of town. Others living in King worked in occupations that supported the company town or were wives and children of the miners.

On January 10, 1893, just before the noon break, an explosion 1,000 feet below the surface, at the sixth level of King Coal Mine No. 5, rocked the stillness of a Tuesday morning. In that instant, nearly a tenth of the King population perished; the official cause was determined to be a lack of judgment by one of the miners who died that day.

Immediately after the explosion, workers on duty quickly made their way to the surface. They met townspeople who had rushed to the mines after the alarm whistle sounded. When the dust settled, and with dozens of miners milling near the sloped No. 5 entrance, a count was taken; seventy-five of the hundred men on duty were unharmed.

One who ran to the surface was Jim Carmosini. He was badly burned and in shock. Soon to be the twenty-fifth victim, Carmosini survived another ten days, likely in severe pain. It was reported in the Golden-based *Colorado Transcript* of February 1, 1893, that after the accident, he never uttered another word.

Another twenty-four miners were missing. Family and friends stood at the slope of the mine "with agonized faces, anxious yet fearful to learn the truth," said the *Flume*. It took two hours before the poisonous air inside was diluted enough for rescuers to enter. Soon after that, it was discovered there were no survivors inside. Bodies were removed and laid side by side in the carpenter shop.

Eleven miners were identified almost immediately, but it took more time to identify the damaged and badly burned bodies of the remaining thirteen. When the extent of the tragedy was known, mine superintendent P. Harding ordered coffins from Denver while recovery continued into the night through a bitter cold snowstorm. The last body was removed in the early morning hours of January 11, 1893.

Of the victims with wives and children, three had families living at King. Robert Blythe left a wife; Stephen Conti left a wife and four children; and Charles Antonelli was survived by his wife and two children.

Site of the King Coal Mine disaster. *Photo taken in April 2015 by the author.*

Blame

On January 12, a coroner's jury (a group summoned to assist a coroner in determining the cause of a person's death) investigated the cause of the explosion. In a unanimous decision, they agreed Union Pacific Coal Company was not to blame. According to the handwritten official report filed in Park County District Court on April 3, 1893, the jury agreed the cause was "the firing of windy [careless] or too heavy shots in room 35 of said mine, which caused an explosion of the mine. We the Jury upon examination of the mine found four shot holes in room 35 from 6 to 8 inches apart."

If the miner did fire four shots, that was too many, according to an explanation of the process by State Mine Inspector John McNeill, published in Boulder's January 13, 1893, *Daily Camera.*

> The sixth level consists of a horizontal tunnel 1700 feet long. Beginning at the 'face' [surface], at regular distances, all the way to the end of the level, there are 'rooms' in which the miners worked. These are excavations on the vein which extend upward from the level, or 'entry,' as it is called, at an angle of 45 degrees, following the coal for 150 to 200 feet. These rooms are numbered in rotation, in the sixth level there are 40 of them.

According to McNeill, before noon each day, miners would break coal from the veins they worked and push it down short stopes (a slanted underground excavation for the removal of ore which is formed as the ore is mined). Then they would load it into cars to be brought to the surface. By noon, each man would also have a hole drilled in the vein, ready to blast out more coal.

Just before noon, each man in each of the forty rooms would have a stick of dynamite ready to fire. The man in room forty would fire his fuse first and the others would follow in order. After each fuse was lit, the men would retreat toward the surface of the mine, where they would break for lunch.

On January 10, the fuses from the first rooms were lit as planned. Something went wrong in room thirty-five; McNeill determined it was due to the carelessness of the miner—first identified as Charles Antonelli and later corrected to Stephen Conti. The explosion didn't happen right away. Fuses were lit in rooms thirty-four through twenty-three before a terrific blast destroyed the sixth level. McNeill said the man in room twenty-three had apparently just lit his fuse and started toward the entry. His body was found in the stope a few feet below his room.

The *Flume* of January 12, 1893, said the air in that part of the mine was allegedly "full of [coal] dust particles ready to be ignited," which may have contributed to the explosion.

When the explanation of "windy" shots hit the news, a rebuttal appeared in the *Flume* of January 26, 1893. Alex Ferrens said he had worked in the King mines for three years and criticized management for employing "ignorant foreigners in preference to English-speaking people."

(His rebuttal seemed to use "ignorant" to mean the inability to speak and read English. Of those killed, the majority were Italians. There is no documentation showing whether they spoke English.)

He said that management had employees, who could not understand English, sign statements written in English acknowledging that any accidents were unavoidable, but, he said, many of the accidents could have been prevented. He said the King No. 5 had been called dangerous by many who had experience in several different mines. He was critical of the procedures for furnishing timbers and the rules for sharpening drills, which, he said, were written only in English. In addition, he questioned the ethics of putting company employees on the coroner's jury, when "there is the possibility of the company being to blame."

The *Flume* seemed to agree with Ferrens when it concluded that "there must have been gas in the mine in quantities to cause so terrible a result."

Burial

According to Allison Chandler in an article, "The Story of Como & King Park, Colorado," in the February 1963 *Denver Westerners Monthly Roundup*, the narrow-gauge train brought the remains to the Catholic church in Como for a mass funeral on Sunday, January 15. The church was too small to bring in all the coffins, so one was brought in to represent all. Some remains had been shipped to the miners' hometowns, but seventeen were slated for Como burial.

After the ceremony, the coffins were taken by train to the Como Cemetery. Two trenches had been dug in the frozen ground large enough for two rows of eight coffins each. As mourners from King paid their last respects, the coffins were lowered, side by side, into the mass grave.

The last coffin, that of Andrew Anderson, a braddish man (one who builds ventilation doors and walls) in the coal mines, was buried separately. The reason, according to Chandler, was that the other victims were Catholics and Anderson was not.

Victims of the January 10, 1893, King Coal Mine disaster were buried at this site in the Como Cemetery. *Photo by the author.*

Translation of the headstone:
"In Memory
Here lies the dead
*[followed by the names
of four Italian miners].*
They died on 10 January 1893
In the mine at King Park, Colo."

The grave is marked by a single headstone, still standing and inscribed with the names of four miners who died in the January 10, 1893, tragedy. In 2015, the headstone was repaired, and a cross, long missing under decades of shifting dirt and aspen leaves, was reattached to the top of the stone. The inscribed names, as they appear on the headstone, follow, showing (in parentheses) how the men were identified in newspapers of the day, and the miner's job assignment at King.

Celeste Corrozzolla di Tres	*(Celeste Corozola)*	*coal digger*
Antonio Tachelini di Carciato	*(Antonio Jackilina)*	*coal digger*
Angelo Giuliani di Malgolo	*(Angelo Juliani)*	*coal digger*
Francesco Pomarolli di Pressero	*(Frank Pomerrolli)*	*braddish man*

Other victims were: Robert Blythe, fire boss; Angelo Dominico, coal digger; Charles K. DeRock, timber man; Peter Ross, timber man; John Toll, tracklayer; Louie Maleringo, entry man; Charles Antonelli, coal digger; Peter Nordina, coal digger; Angelo Marino, coal digger; Joseph Donna, coal digger; Michael Richi, coal digger; Donatte de French, entry man; Stephen Conti, coal digger; Antone Pretti, coal digger; Antonio Antonelli, coal digger; Thomas K. Ross, coal digger; Michael Antonelli, coal digger; Joseph Schrioda, coal digger; and Joseph Diajackamo (also known as Joseph James), entry man.

The twenty-fifth casualty, James Carmosini, died on January 20, ten days after the explosion. He is also buried at Como.

Strike

One week after the blast, one hundred men from the King Coal Mine went on strike, complaining that the mine was unsafe. The *Flume* said, "The trouble will probably be satisfactorily adjusted."

And apparently it was. A story in the January 25, 1893, *Silver Cliff Rustler* reported a plan to have all the shots at the King mine fired by one man, who would be selected by the miners. By selecting the man considered by the majority to be most competent, it was expected future accidents would be prevented.

More Accidents

In February 1893, Fortunati Pedre died when a large mass of clay fell from a wall and broke his neck and thigh. It was determined by the coroner's jury that "the accident was entirely accidental, for which no one was responsible." In March 1893, two Italian miners were severely burned in a dust explosion. It was first reported that they were expected to live. Both died a few days later.

By fall, the accidents were all but forgotten. The *Flume* of September 28, 1893, reported, "The coal mines at King are at work again and sending out the usual amount of coal." But small accidents continued to happen, including two injuries to mine superintendent Harding in February and April 1894.

By 1900, the mines were shut down, and the town was abandoned, although coal was sporadically mined at the King site into the 1930s. Remaining at the mine site today are brick and stone foundations, the mine dumps, a few pieces of metal, and the sealed mines. No buildings remain from the town.

Chapter 11

King City

Nearly Forgotten

T he coal-mining community of King City, located about three miles southeast of present-day Como, was short lived. It is best known for the tragic coal mine explosion that occurred there in 1893. Then in its fourteenth year, the town lasted another three years after the explosion, until 1896, when its post office closed for good.

King City circa the 1890s. *Park County Local History Archives, Brisbois Photo—Leadville, Bob Schoppe Collection.*

Italian miners settled the area in April 1879. The town grew to a high population of about 400 after immigrants from China and five European nations joined the few Americans digging coal for the railroad.

King was situated between rolling hills covered in grass, sage, and wildflowers. Because there were few trees, residents enjoyed excellent views of the fourteen-thousand-foot peaks of the Continental Divide. A few miles from town was Lake Como, occupying a deep depression between windswept hills. Previous generations of area children used to skate on the lake in winter, but it rarely holds water today. When it does, the shallow summer depth provides a haven for migrating water birds.

King City, also called King Park and King, was a sister city to Como. Their histories intertwined; they even shared a name for a while—the difference was that Como survived.

Coal Discovery

King got its start in 1876 when three coalfields were discovered in the area. The first was found by Stubbs Ranch owner George Lechner. Called the Upper Mine, it was about a mile northwest of present-day Como. Lechner sold the coal locally for ten dollars per ton.

At about the same time, two coalfields were discovered at the future site of King by a man named George Boyd. Those mines were interchangeably called the Lower Como Mines, the Boyd Mines, and (later) the King Mines. They were located in Park Gulch, south of present-day Elkhorn Road (County Road 15) at the north end of South Park. The three small veins covered about twenty-three square miles; the most profitable of the group was King Mine No. 5, not far from the town of King.

The King and Como mines produced semibituminous coal, an intermediate grade, ranked between soft bituminous and the hardest and highest-quality, anthracite. The mined product was soft and crumbly, as is evident in the small pieces that still dot the King mine site today. The coal was especially well-suited for steam locomotives and power plants, according to a study by the Sixty-Third Congress in 1914.

As a result of the three discoveries, The South Park Coal Company (of which the Denver, South Park & Pacific Railroad, or DSP&P, owned 87.5 percent) was formed in April 1879, with ownership that encompassed the three fields. In

1880, when the Union Pacific Railroad took over operations of the DSP&P, the company name was changed to the Union Pacific Coal Company.

The First "Como"

When the lower mines opened in April 1879, the early arriving Italian miners named the nearby body of water Lake Como, after a beautiful lake in their homeland, and called their town Como. The name didn't last long. In June of that year, the end of the DSP&P track was about three miles to the northwest of the lower mines, at the present site of Como. There, a depot and roundhouse were built, and railroad officials called the depot "Como," possibly because that was the name of the nearest settlement.

As was typical, a town sprang up near the depot and roundhouse, and that town was also called Como. That's when the name of the lower town was changed to King. It was named after Adolph J. (Jim) King, a two-term Park County clerk and recorder who managed the coal mines there. He was also proprietor of the store at King and ran the post office inside the store.

In addition to the store, other businesses included four livery stables, a blacksmith shop, a carpenter shop, one saloon, a combination school and church, a wooden water tank, and, near the edge of town, a livestock pen. The mine company also had a powder house for storage of explosives and a scale house for weighing coal. Residents occupied sixty light-colored frame houses laid out on either side of the street. Some sources say there was a cemetery at King; however, it has not been found. Some deceased residents from King are buried at the Como Cemetery.

Miners' Dispute

There were some disputes between the different nationalities that lived and worked at King City, chiefly between the Italian and the Chinese workers. Both were considered lower class by American and British miners, resulting in segregated housing.

The Americans and British occupied the south end of town. Germans, Italians, Austrians, and Hungarians lived on the north end. It is believed by historians that the Chinese miners lived at the 1859-era placer-mining towns of Hamilton and Tarryall City, north of current day Como on Tarryall Creek. That site is approximately five miles away from King. (All traces of Hamilton and Tarryall City were buried during dredging operations in the 1940s.)

Few Reminders

In about 1896, the post office closed. Some buildings were dismantled and moved to the present site of Como; some were demolished for lumber and firewood. Within a few years, no trace remained of the town.

The mismatched and tattered shoes shown above are some of the few remaining artifacts from King. They were picked up at the townsite by a private collector several years ago and returned to Como in November 2015. As of May 2016, they are on display at Como's Mountain Man Gallery. *Photo by the author.*

Chapter 12

Balfour

A Dream That Died

In early 1893, Park County was losing population. The entire nation was in a depression. It was the year that Congress repealed the Sherman Silver Purchase Act, meaning US currency was no longer based on the bimetallism of silver and gold, but was based solely on gold. The result was a huge drop in the price of silver, and, although gold prices increased, it was a rough time for Park County's mining industry.

Then, in November 1893, gold was discovered in a seemingly unlikely place and at an opportune time. Existing public records do not specify who made the initial discovery, but the find attracted immediate attention in Park County's financially depressed economy. The discovery was on one hundred and sixty acres of a former sheep ranch nestled in the rolling grasslands of South Park.

The new gold field, nine miles south of Hartsel, was promoted as having the same mineral content as Cripple Creek (in adjacent Teller County), where gold was discovered in 1890 and is still mined in 2016. A town grew in the midst of the promised gold; it was called Balfour.

Buffalo Slough

Anticipating a gold rush, the Balfour Town & Improvement Company was formed in November 1893 by Henry B. Gillespie and Byron E. Shear, Aspen silver tycoons, and H. J. Putnam. Gillespie was named company president, and

Adolphe J. (Jim) King—the former storekeeper in King City—was named secretary. Their goal was to secure title to the land and to plat a townsite.

Official Seal of the Balfour Town & Improvement Company, 1893. *Park County Local History Archives.*

The discovery came at just the right time for Gillespie. He was an Aspen, Colorado, businessman experienced in mining. Before coming to Balfour, he had owned Aspen's Mollie Gibson Mine and then had managed it for its subsequent owner, John J. Hagerman. It was the richest silver mine in the world, according to an 1892 book, *The Silver Dollar: A Business View*, by Edward Frederick Browne. When the bottom fell out of the silver market in the summer of 1893, Gillespie, who also had experience as a town promoter, was fortunate to find a new area to promote in southern South Park.

The 1893 discovery wasn't the first time gold had been mined in the area. The first prospecting there was in 1866, and, sporadically for the next few decades, some gold was found. In 1885, E. O. "Obe" Fyffe, a sheep rancher and owner of the future site of Balfour, then called the Buffalo Sloughs, reported that "a number of prospectors" were working the land in the district and finding good gold, according to the March 12, 1885, *Flume*. (A "slough" is an area of soft, muddy ground.)

The gold discovery might have made Fyffe a rich man, but by 1893, he was no longer in control of his land. Two years earlier, Fyffe had been convicted of the second-degree murder of A. C. Scribner, a neighboring sheep rancher. They had had a dispute over a fence line, according to the July 7, 1891, *Aspen Daily Chronicle*. In 1893, Fyffe was serving a thirty-year sentence in the state penitentiary in Cañon City.

Fyffe had lost possession of his ranch, and Gillespie, King, and the other company directors—some of whom had come from Aspen with Gillespie, others of whom had come from Denver—wanted it. At the time, the property was in control of an assignee, the Denver branch of Salina, Kansas-based Crippen, Lawrence and Company, negotiators in real estate mortgages. In November 1893, by court agreement, Crippen, Lawrence and Company had secured title to the land and they had then sold it to the Balfour Town & Improvement Company. On December 23, 1893, the Balfour town plat was approved by Park County, and town lots went up for sale.

The names Crippen and Lawrence are significant because when the town was platted, two streets were named Crippen and Lawrence. The names showed up in other town documents as well. A Mr. Lawrence owned one of the mines, and J. J. Crippen was a company director, likely the same Joseph J. Crippen who was a principal in the firm of Crippen, Lawrence and Company.

Balfour Begins

The town grew quickly. The first *Balfour News*, dated January 20, 1894, reported that when Gillespie and King arrived at the future townsite on December 2, 1893, a few scattered tents and the old sheep rancher's cabin were the only structures. Within ten days, if notations on old photographs are correct, a town was born, with several frame cabins replacing the tents. By the end of January, town business was being conducted from a "handsome frame office structure," reported the paper.

It didn't take long for the news to spread. By the time the town was two months old, eight hundred people were living at Balfour. Seventeen mines were mentioned in that first *Balfour News*, and it said plans were being made to open a post office, a general store, and a livery barn. The company was selling lots at a fast pace, and the buildings being erected were of "substantial character indicating the faith of the builders in the permanency and future growth of Balfour," the paper boasted. By March 1894, both the *Buena Vista Herald* in Chaffee County and the *Silver Cliff Rustler* in Custer County were reporting a population of one thousand in Balfour with "hotel accommodations of a superior order for a new camp."

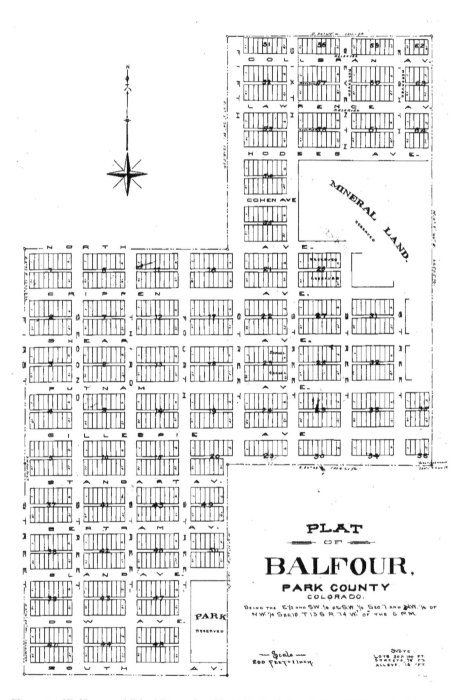

Plat map of Balfour, established December 23, 1893. *Park County Local History Archives.*

Balfour could save South Park's depressed economy, or at least that was what many believed. In Buena Vista's December 20, 1893, *Colorado Democrat*, it was reported that the surface indications at Balfour "are much more promising than they were in the Cripple Creek District." And the first edition of the town paper reported that "Balfour will take its place among the steady gold producers of the state."

It seemed too good to be true.

Growth

In March 1894, Fairplay merchant Samuel Cohen opened a store in Balfour. In the first six months of 1894, more businesses opened: a mining and milling company, at least three hotels, an undertaker/furniture maker, and another store with an attached bakery. Also, the post office was established—with A. J. King as postmaster—the town was incorporated, and a chamber of commerce and bureau of information were established. Stages ran from Cañon City and from Spinney, and a railroad was nine miles away at Hartsel.

A school was opened in March 1894 with twenty-five pupils. Four months later, in July 1894, Balfour had the fifth-highest enrollment of school children of the twenty-four districts in the county, with thirty-nine enrolled. The South Park-area districts with more pupils than Balfour in July 1894 were Alma (127), Como (108), Fairplay (92), and King (49).

Five and a half years later, in October 1899, the Balfour School was discontinued by the county commissioners until such time as "there were fifteen children of school age to attend." It did not reopen.

Mining

The Hartsel Gold Mining District, which was centered on Balfour, was established in November 1893, and in January 1894, a miner's organization, or union, was formed at Balfour. It was agreed that miners would earn $3 for each eight-hour day. And, to prevent the disagreements such as those that occurred at Como and King, it was agreed that anyone of Chinese or Italian ancestry would not be allowed in the camp. That motion carried "amidst great cheering," reported the January 18, 1894, *Flume*.

There were some who doubted the value of gold at Balfour. To convince everyone that the town was the site of a viable gold-mining operation, a banner was attached to the rail car carrying the first assay sample to Denver. It proudly announced "the first car load of gold ore from Balfour mining camp," according to the February 13, 1894, *Aspen Daily Times* in a reprinted story from the *Balfour News*. The banner and accompanying streamers, as well as the results of the assay, "will open the eyes of the unbelievers," the newspaper reported.

Gold from the richest mine in the district, the Ella C, assayed at forty dollars to the ton in its first carload, which Buena Vista's *Colorado Democrat* reported as "pretty good for a maiden effort."

(This assay of the Ella C compared well to the historic mines in Mosquito Gulch near Alma, where assays averaged from twenty-five dollars to eighty dollars per ton in gold and silver, according to the April 28, 1881, *Flume*.)

In March 1894, reports showed increased assay results, and a story in the March 27, 1894, *Aspen Daily Times* said wire gold (thin fragile strands of gold in the shape of wire) was discovered at the Ella C that assayed at $413 per ton. More good news was reported in the Denver-based trade publication the *Daily Mining Record* of May 10, 1894, when it told of the findings of Benjamin Sadtler, a professor of metallurgy and mineralogy at the Colorado State School of Mines (now the Colorado School of Mines) in Golden.

Sadtler said the geological conditions at Balfour and at Cripple Creek "are essentially the same" and that the Balfour camp "would seem to promise equally well." He clarified that by continuing: "This, however, can only be finally determined by further development, as not enough has yet been done to determine finally the degree of mineralization, although what results have been obtained are exceedingly promising." The article said that out of 400 samples assayed, "the large majority showed from a trace upwards of gold."

Sadtler said an assayer named Mr. Snyder had obtained assays from $2.40 to nearly $6,000 per ton. Another assayer, a Mr. Briggs, had results in "various amounts, although none quite as high as Mr. Snyder's highest." Sadtler concluded that "with proper development, the future of the camp should be bright." He based his conclusion on the presence of mineralization geologically similar to that of Cripple Creek and on the presence of well-defined veins.

Dream Dies

But the expectations and dreams of profitable gold mining were never realized at Balfour. Even from the beginning, news reports alternated back and forth, with conflicting accounts of Balfour's riches. Buena Vista's *Colorado Democrat* may have spoken for the region when it said in its December 18, 1893, edition, "The newspaper reports of Balfour make one's head ache."

The good-news stories outnumbered the bad until, on November 22, 1894, one of the last optimistic newspaper reports about Balfour was published. The *Flume* reprinted a *Balfour News* item that said, "Balfour is in a better condition at present to boom than ever before in the history of the camp." Still, it didn't boom. Little more was printed about the dying town until March 27, 1896, when the *Aspen Daily Times* reported, "The Balfour mining camp—a region that experienced an excitement two years ago over gold discoveries that never materialized the gold—is now totally deserted."

Even that wasn't quite true. It wasn't until February 1, 1906, nearly 10 years after that story, that stage service and the mail route from Hartsel to Balfour was discontinued and the post office was closed, according to the January 16, 1906, *Flume*. And there were still people living in Balfour over a year later. The second-to-the-last resident recorded in history died on July 14, 1907. She was Mary Morse, who had lived with her surviving husband in the otherwise deserted Balfour for years. She is buried at the Hartsel Cemetery.

Balfour's final mention in the *Flume* as an operational town was on December 3, 1915, when the Park County delinquent tax list showed Balfour properties for the last time.

In the end, the reason Balfour died, said Aspen's *Rocky Mountain Sun* on December 24, 1898, was "for want of that important requisite to a successful mineral camp—mineral."

1900s–1910s

Chapter 13

Pre-1906 Miracle Medicines

Mystery Ingredients: Morphine, Alcohol, and Heroin

Morphine was the primary ingredient of Mrs. Winslow's Soothing Syrup for teething infants; it also contained alcohol. The product was available from about 1865 until about 1913 in the United States and until about 1930 in Europe.

Mrs. Winslow's Soothing Syrup advertisement. *Miami U. Libraries digital collections via Wikimedia Commons Public Domain.*

A colorful advertisement from the nineteenth century shows a loving mother cuddled in bed with her children reading about Mrs. Winslow's syrup. Other ads show a happy, smiling mother and baby playing in the morning after a full night's sleep, thanks to the soothing syrup, and a mother surrounded by her supportive older children as she gives the baby a dose of teething medication.

What the ads didn't say is that sometimes the baby never woke up.

The syrup was responsible for the death of many infants, even when taking the recommended dosage, according to the Food and Drug Administration at www.fda.gov. It could be purchased in drugstores throughout the United States, including Park County, as indicated by advertisements in the *Flume* from 1897 to 1913: "Mrs. Winslow's Soothing Syrup. For children teething, softens the gums, reduces inflammation, allays pain, cures wind colic, 25 cents a bottle."

Ingredients Not Listed

There was no labeling requirement on medicine containers before 1906, and druggists' shelves were stocked with so-called medical cures later found to contain heroin, morphine, alcohol, and other harmful drugs. They were all available without a prescription. Consumers had no idea what was in the medicines on the druggists' shelves. Druggists and newspaper editors who ran advertisements for the drugs may not have known either.

In 1906, a law was passed by the Fifty-Ninth Congress called the Pure Food and Drug Act. Among other regulations, it required that medicine containers include a full list of ingredients. It was a start. Medicines could still contain any ingredient as long as it was listed on the label. And the law only pertained to interstate sales. If, for example, a drug was manufactured in Colorado and sold in Colorado, the law didn't apply.

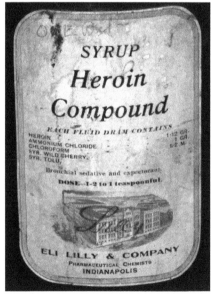

Heroin was available over the counter until 1920. *Photo by the author.*

One product sold after 1906 was Eli Lilly's Heroin Compound. It was a "bronchial sedative and expectorant" and also contained wild cherry flavoring and chloroform (used as an anesthetic until about 1900, when it was found to hasten death). Eli Lilly, however, wasn't the first company to market heroin.

Bayer Heroin

Heroin was invented in 1874 by an English chemist, but it was the German chemist Heinrich Dreser, an employee of Bayer Pharmaceutical Products of Germany, who saw its potential. In 1898, he began marketing Bayer Heroin. The name came from Bayer workers, who, following experiments made before the drug was released, said it made them feel "heroic."

Dreser was marketing two drugs in 1898 for the Bayer Company. The other was aspirin, called the world's most successful legal drug in an online article about heroin history at www.opioids.com. It called heroin the world's most successful illegal drug.

With heroin, Dreser was looking for a nonaddictive substitute for morphine, widely used at that time as a painkiller and treatment for respiratory disease. He offered heroin as a cough medicine that was ten times more effective than codeine with one-tenth the toxic effects. He also said it was a more effective and safer painkiller than morphine.

Heroin was seen as a miracle medicine, and it was invented at a time when there was a high demand for reliable respiratory medicines. In the late 1890s, the two leading causes of death by disease were tuberculosis and pneumonia, both respiratory ailments. Heroin was later found to be highly addictive, and Bayer stopped making it in 1913.

Early 'Medical Miracles'

A variety of medicinal cures were available to the unsuspecting public in the late 1800s and early 1900s; one could find products that claimed to cure just about any ailment.

Celery Nervine

There was Celery Nervine, from the Smith-Dunkley Company in Kalamazoo, Michigan. The company's advertising said it was the largest of the celery shippers in the United States. It sold canned celery, pickled celery, fresh celery, and a product called Celery Nervine.

The drug was promoted as a blood and nerve tonic for "the relief and cure of nervous disorders for the blood and brain," according to labels on the box. It was promoted as "a boon to anyone afflicted with nervousness or stomach troubles," its ad said. It also relieved restlessness, insomnia, and was helpful for a stomach that needed toning up. One could buy it at the Owl Drug Store in Fairplay.

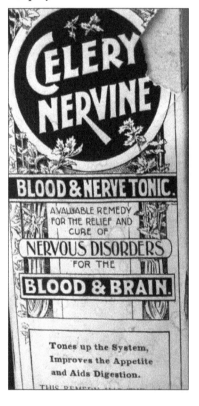

Nervine was a concoction made by other manufacturers besides the Kalamazoo-based company. They weren't all made with celery, but they were all often sold as treatments for exhaustion, epilepsy, spasms, fits, pain, and depression. The active ingredient was bromide, formerly used as a sedative until it was discovered that excessive use could cause psychiatric, neurological, gastrointestinal, and skin disorders. But one wouldn't know that from seeing an advertisement for the product. It featured two women talking on the phone. One asked what the loud noise was in the background of the other woman's line. The second woman explained, "Oh! That's the children playing—since I have been taking Nervine nothing bothers me."

Celery Nervine. *Photo by the author.*

Lydia Pinkham's Herb Medicine

A medicine that was advertised extensively in the *Flume* and throughout the country was Lydia Pinkham's Herb Medicine. The label clearly stated, almost apologetically, that it contained fifteen percent alcohol, but it was "added solely as a solvent and preservative." The Pinkham tonic claimed to treat a variety of women's reproductive problems by a compound of several herbs, according to

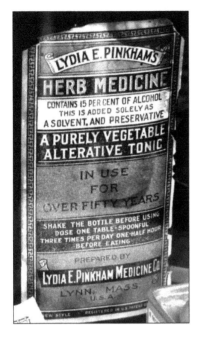

www.lydiapinkham.org. The primary ingredient was black cohosh, native to the United States and known as the woman's herb. The vegetable tonic, with minor changes, is still used today, and with success, according to the website.

Lydia Pinkham's Herb Medicine. *Photo by the author.*

Fink's Magic Oil

Henry George Greatrake Fink was a clergyman from Ohio who discovered that the patent medicine business was a much easier way to make a living. He made Fink's Magic Oil, a cure-all for aches and pains and other maladies such as mumps, asthma, ringworm, and a condition called cholera morbus. Its symptoms were severe cramps, diarrhea, and vomiting. The magic oil cured it all. Or at least one felt cured. And it probably did take away the pain; it was eighty-seven percent alcohol.

Fink's Magic Oil. *Photo by the author.*

Holman's Ague, Liver and Stomach Pad

This was a pad that was placed on the pit of one's stomach, where the ribs begin to separate. It was held in place by straps around the neck and a belt around the chest. There was no medicine in the bag, just absorbing material. It was said to remove poison from the body. To cure ague (illness with fever and shaking) as well as liver and stomach problems, one wore the bag for four to six weeks continuously and then one week per month between April and November and at any other time when symptoms were present. The pad could not be used for more than one season or by more than one person.

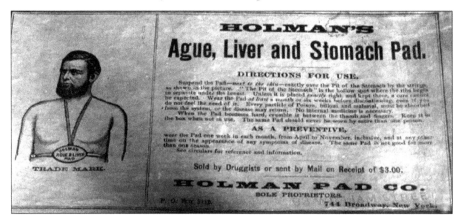

Holman's Ague, Liver and Stomach Pad. *Photo by the author.*

Hamlins Wizard Oil

Hamlins Wizard Oil was well marketed. The company sponsored singing troupes known as the Wizard Oil Concert Companies. They held concerts, passed out songbooks to the audience, and sang songs that told about the diseases Hamlins Wizard Oil would cure. The medicine attested to curing a long list of physical problems: stiffness and soreness anywhere on the body, deafness, sprains, animal bites, diphtheria (an upper respiratory tract illness), dyspepsia (indigestion), bleeding gums, and ulcers. It was advertised regularly in the *Flume* in 1901 and 1902.

The ads said the product was for internal and external use and featured testimony of the product's "wonderful healing powers" from "hundreds of supposed cripples for life." A list of ingredients is topped by alcohol at sixty-five

percent, plus oil camphor (removed from the US market in the 1980s for safety concerns), oil thyme (germ killer), oil cajeput (treats colds, headaches, tumors), oil sassafras (today used in the illicit manufacture of the drug ecstasy), oil fir (used for muscle aches and pains), gum camphor (made from turpentine, used in rubs and salves), turpentine, capsicum (treats digestive problems), and ammonia.

Hamlins Wizard Oil Liniment. *Photo by the author.*

Warner's Safe Diabetes Remedy. *Photo by the author.*

Warner's Safe Diabetes Cure and Remedy

Warner's Safe Remedies Company of Rochester, New York, made many so-called safe cures and remedies—for diabetes, for the liver and kidney, and for rheumatic fever. Typically, a medicine was labeled as a "cure" before the 1906 Pure Food and Drug Act. With the passage of the act and the resultant truth in labeling, many cures were then labeled as remedies. Warner's history includes both cures and remedies. It was advertised as a treatment to stop diabetes if one began taking the medicine in time. But that claim was false; neither the cure nor the remedy could control or stop diabetes.

Patent Medicines

The medicines mentioned in this chapter and hundreds of others that were available to consumers in the years before 1906 were called patent medicines. They were medicines that promised cures, but those promises were not backed by science. There were no restrictions on advertising, and manufacturers were not required to list ingredients. Addiction by consumers to heroin, morphine, and alcohol was common.

There were physicians and medical societies that disagreed with the use of patent medicines, according to an article on the history of patent medicine at www.hagley.org, a website of the Hagley (Delaware) Museum and Library. Those doctors were critical of the hazardous ingredients and resultant drug dependency of their patients. On the other hand, a trade association of medicine producers fought the Pure Food and Drug Act; they were aided by the press, which had grown dependent on patent medicine advertising dollars.

The act was passed by Congress in 1906 with strong support from President Theodore Roosevelt and went into law on January 1, 1907.

Chapter 14

1916 to 1919

Not the Good Old Days

Ah, the good old days. Life was better back then, or so it's been said. But maybe not in the years from 1916 to 1919. Then, the "good old days" seemed pretty bad.

World War I started, and in Park County and throughout the nation men as young as eighteen were drafted and sent to European battlefields in 1917 and 1918. The lives of some were claimed by warfare, but about half of the fatalities were attributed to Spanish influenza that raced through the trenches of Europe.

Other soldiers never made it to Europe; they died in US training bases where influenza spread through the barracks. The flu of 1918 was called the "most devastating epidemic in recorded world history" in a story on the Stanford University website; it claimed more lives worldwide than the war. It also hit Park County.

And before the United States entered World War I and the influenza pandemic officially started, Colorado became one of the first states to ratify Prohibition, making it illegal to manufacture, import, advertise, or keep for sale or gift, any intoxicating liquors. The measure did not specifically prohibit alcohol use or drunkenness, although its design was meant to limit both by making alcohol difficult to obtain. It was thought Prohibition would put an end to crime, poverty, and violence. Instead, they increased, and the added costs to enforce the law were high.

Prohibition

A new year typically brings new laws, and in January 2014 two states—Colorado and Washington—were the first to legalize recreational marijuana. In Colorado, the majority vote on November 6, 2012, was 55.3 percent. That's a near reversal from Election Day, November 3, 1914, when, in a 52.3 percent majority, Colorado joined Washington and Oregon in outlawing alcohol.

In Colorado, Prohibition was effective January 1, 1916. Other states had become dry in preceding years, and by 1920, it was made a national law by passage of the 18th Amendment to the US Constitution. Prohibition lasted for almost seventeen and a half years in Colorado, until July 1, 1933, when voters passed Article 22 of the state constitution. It repealed Prohibition within the state's borders. Nationally, Prohibition was repealed on December 5, 1933, following passage of the 21st Amendment.

STATE-WIDE PROHIBITION AN INJURY TO TEMPERANCE

The *Flume* fought hard against Prohibition before the 1914 election, beginning in September 1914 and continuing through October 30, 1914, the last edition before the November 3 election. It used the likenesses of former presidents Theodore Roosevelt and Abraham Lincoln and anti-Prohibition quotes from clergymen from across the United States in an effort to sway voters against the amendment.

A bishop from Vermont gave a prophetic opinion in the October 30, 1914, *Flume*, when he said, "Prohibition drives underground the mischief which it seeks to cure, making it more difficult to deal with the evil and impossible to regulate the trade."

Anti-Prohibition advertisement in the October 16, 1914, *Flume. Clip courtesy of Colorado Historic Newspapers, www.coloradohistoricnewspapers.org.*

But the amendment did pass. The Senate and Board of Trade saloons—both in Fairplay—advertised for the last time in the *Flume* of December 31, 1915. It was the final day one could legally buy alcohol in Colorado for over seventeen years (with the exception of use for medicinal and sacramental purposes). In the years from 1917 to 1920, an exception to the Colorado Prohibition Amendment allowed households to import for personal use up to two quarts of whiskey, six quarts of wine, or twenty-four quarts of beer per month, but even that went away with national Prohibition.

Senate Saloon on Front Street in Fairplay, Colorado, late 1800s. *Park County Local History Archives, South Park Historical Foundation, Charles Markle photo.*

Ironically, after the law was in force in Colorado, the *Flume* had no local coverage of its effect in the county, with the exception of one sentence in the January 7, 1916, edition. "Alma is without a marshal now since the saloons are closed," it said, apparently indicating that no laws would be broken without alcohol to fuel the crimes. One might conclude that alcohol was no longer a part of Park County life.

Or one could read the oral histories that old-timers recorded for the Park County Local History Archives for another slant on the Prohibition years.

In Park County

"Well, there were several bootleggers," said Andy Anderson in a 2005 interview about growing up in Como. He was born in 1920 and repeated stories from his father and grandfather, and he related some from his own memories. He said that the richest man in town was the bootlegger.

Anderson talked about George and Sadie Duffey, who lived in the area of the Como Cemetery and today's Camp Como. They made and sold moonshine and "the feds were always coming out of Denver . . . and they were always after George." But they rarely caught him. A worker on the train would send a message to the Como station saying the "feds were on the train." So the Duffeys usually had fair warning and hid the moonshine.

Jim Gardner (1950-2006), the late Park County commissioner whose family has lived in the area since 1919, was interviewed in 2002 for the Park County Local History Archives. He said, "There were bootleggers out the Elkhorn, too," in reference to Elkhorn Road, also known as County Road 15.

Gardner talked about Como bootleggers as well:

> Como was a dying railroad town, even by the early '20s—still had gaslights, still had sidewalks, still had four or five saloons before prohibition shut them down . . . but then they had a lot of bootleggers.

Merrill Wright from Jefferson was also interviewed in 2002. He was born in 1923 and remembers what happened when his dad would "get with all the guys, and they'd get a few drinks and start trying to sing" during Prohibition days.

"They'd get lit, and I tell you, it was something else. They thought they could really sing, and the more they'd drink, why the louder they sang," he said.

Shortly after the Colorado Prohibition law was passed, the United States went to war.

World War I

World War I began in 1914, but it didn't affect the nation and Park County significantly until April 6, 1917, when the United States joined the Allies, whose major countries included France, Britain, and Russia, in declaration of war on the Central Powers of Germany, the Austrian-Hungarian Empire, the Ottoman Empire (Turkey), and Bulgaria. Six weeks later, on May 18, 1917, an act of Congress gave the president the power to draft men into military service. It was called the Selective Service Act (still used as of 2016 with modifications). It required men between the ages of twenty-one and thirty to register. By September 1918, men from eighteen to forty-five were being drafted.

Park County residents heeded the call.

"The county seat was very busy Wednesday, there being a number of people from the various towns bringing in returns of the registration for the selective draft," reported the June 8, 1917, *Flume*.

In that same issue, a chart showed that of the 278 men of "fighting age" living in Park County, the greatest number were from Fairplay, with eighty men, followed by Guffey and Jefferson, each with twenty-eight men. Other towns represented included Bailey, with thirteen men; Como, with fourteen; Grant, five; Lake George, fifteen; Hartsel, twelve; and Alma, eighteen.

Among the first to be drafted from Park County, on September 19, 1917, was Fred H. Hammond of Guffey. Along with other draftees from Park County, he was sent to Camp Funston in northeastern Kansas, a US Army training center within the Fort Riley military reservation. His mother received two letters from him when he was at the camp.

Hammond told her in the first letter that he was hospitalized and convalescing from an attack of measles. In the next letter, he said he wasn't doing so well, according to the December 14, 1917, *Flume*.

He never made it to Europe and the war. In mid-December 1917, Hammond's parents received word that his death on December 9 was caused by pneumonia, a complication of the measles.

Hammond's remains were sent to Cañon City, Colorado, where he was "the first soldier dying in the Great War to be brought (there)," said the December 21, 1917, *Flume*. On the day of his military-honors funeral at Cañon City's Greenwood Cemetery, flags were flown at half-staff throughout town. His remains lay in state for two hours at the YMCA building, where "hundreds of people marched past his coffin, which was draped with the American Flag and almost obscured by masses of beautiful flowers."

Fred Henry Hammond, 1917. *Photo courtesy of Doug Stiverson.*

Hammond, engaged to marry Mildred Hewitt of Cascade, Colorado, at the time he was drafted, was a tall twenty-two-year-old farmer of medium build. He had gray eyes and brown hair, according to his draft card. The son of Henry and Fannie Hammond, he lived and worked on the Bender Ranch north of Guffey, his lifelong home. Fred's father, Henry Hammond, had a sister, Annie Hammond Bender. The ranch was named for Annie and her husband, John Bender, according to Doug Stiverson, a descendant of the Hammond and Bender families. (As of 2016, it was the Aspen Creek Ranch and a designated Park County historic landmark since 2007.)

Had Hammond been sent to Camp Funston six months later, in March 1918, he would have found the camp in the midst of one of the first Spanish influenza outbreaks in the 1918 to 1919 pandemic.

Spanish Influenza

There is speculation that the pandemic began at Camp Funston, where all draftees first reported and from where they were deployed to fight the war, according to the website of the National Center for Biotechnology Information. But scientists do not know for certain where it started. Unofficial death estimates, as reported in the October 11, 1918, *Flume*, was one death in every twenty-seven cases. More recent information at the Centers for Disease Control and Prevention website estimates the number of deaths in the pandemic at thirty million to fifty million worldwide, including 675,000 in the United States.

Gathering in groups, even watching a children's baseball game, was avoided in 1918-1919 to prevent the flu from spreading. Shown here is the Fairplay team of 1905. *Park County Local History Archives, Source: Maxine Heberer Manewal.*

Colorado population centers complied with Governor Julius Gunter's direction and took steps to limit the spread of the disease. In Fairplay, the board of trustees ordered that all schools, theaters, churches, and other places where people assembled be closed until further notice. Parents were urged to avoid the gathering of children in homes, and citizens were asked to stay home if feeling ill, even from a cold, until "the nature of their illness (is) determined," said the October 11, 1918, *Flume*.

But still, there were from one to three influenza or pneumonia deaths reported in the *Flume* each week in the fall of 1918. Most were young, healthy adult men, including Leroy Merrill Wright, twenty-eight, a soldier from Jefferson; Alfred Turner, a soldier, age unknown, of Garo; and Cecil Dewey Stephens, twenty, a Fairplay resident. Women were also affected. Albertina Almgren, forty-four, died in Boulder in October 1918. She had recently moved there from Fairplay, her home for fifteen years. She is buried at the Fairplay Cemetery.

By the summer of 1919, the flu pandemic came to an end, because, according to www.history.com, "those that were infected either died or developed immunity." In 2008, researchers discovered why the 1918 flu virus was so deadly. It was determined that "a group of three genes enabled the virus to weaken a victim's bronchial tubes and lungs and clear the way for bacterial pneumonia."

1920s–1930s

Chapter 15

Historic Halloween

Pranks, Parties, Myths

It was probably all in fun, but the fun ended with a gunshot wound to the head for fifteen-year-old Colorado Springs high school student Archie Tolley on October 31, 1922. The *Flume* of November 17, 1922, said Archie was with a group of other boys when one of them threw a firecracker into Alexander Meredith's Colorado Springs yard.

Meredith's response was to fire a shotgun at the group; Archie was hit in the head and face. He was seriously injured, but there was no follow-up story to let readers know if he survived. It seems possible he did. A veterinarian named Archibald Douglas Tolley died in Colorado Springs in 1969; he was born in 1906 and was listed as a thirteen-year-old living in Colorado Springs in the 1920 United States Census. The sixty-three-year-old Tolley in 1969 could very well have been the injured Halloween prankster of 1922.

Pranks Expected

Halloween pranks by youth were seemingly expected in the years around the turn of the twentieth century. The November 2, 1917, *Flume* reported that Fairplay showed signs that the younger citizens were out in force on October 31 because "all the vehicles could be seen scattered over the streets of our town."

One can imagine a group of youth out on Halloween, often in the snow, pushing unsecured cars, wagons, and buggies from one end of town to the other—probably a noisy activity, with much shouting and yelling. The youthful mischief was apparently accepted for many years. The *Buena Vista Democrat* of November 7, 1890, reported that Halloween saw the usual celebrating "by the boys, in removing gates, boxes, etc., from their usual moorings."

Removing gates was a popular activity for young people on Halloween through the years. A story in Buena Vista's October 30, 1895, *Chaffee County Republican* reminded residents that it would be Halloween the next day and to "look after your gates."

Occasionally town authorities would intervene to stop childish Halloween pranks. The November 3, 1905, *Flume* reported the tamest Halloween celebration in years and said it was because "the marshal had the boys pretty well frightened." That year there were few pranks on Halloween night. But maybe the tame Halloween had more to do with the foot of snow that fell between Sunday, October 29, and Tuesday, October 31, than with the marshal's threat.

Sometimes pranks went too far. The November 7, 1924, *Chaffee County Republican* reported extreme Halloween damage that year. It conceded that "pranks are pranks, and Halloween pranks are often overlooked, supposed to have been done by small boys and little children," but damage during the 1924 Halloween in Buena Vista was not done by children, the paper said.

A large window of the post office was broken, two wheels of a large wagon were pushed through its door, and the floor was littered with paper. The Hotel Princeton was extensively damaged, and stores in town had piles of ashes left at doorsteps, and their windows were marked with soap. Vehicles were overturned, including a buggy at the telephone office and a large wagon at the Hotel Princeton. A bicycle was put on top of a telephone sign, and the weighing scales from the Central Drug Store were found at the barbershop across the street.

And, "of course," the paper said, "many gates were missing."

Park County Pranks

In the 1930s, indoor plumbing was not common, at least not in Park County. Behind every home there was an outhouse. And they were prime targets for pranks on Halloween.

Andy Anderson grew up in Como and graduated from Como High School in the late 1930s. He was interviewed by a volunteer with the Park County Local History Archives on September 29, 2005. During the interview, he said kids in Como "were kind of ornery around Halloween sometimes." He said, "They (apparently not including himself in the group) turned over outhouses hoping to get somebody in there. They put a buggy on top of the (elementary) schoolhouse."

When asked where the buggy came from, Anderson said that "they" found it somewhere. It was "one somebody had in their garage there."

Budde Freeman grew up in Fairplay and graduated from Fairplay High School in the early 1940s. She was interviewed on September 12, 2002, by a member of the Park County Archives. Freeman said there were Halloween parties when she was younger, but as kids got older, it was more fun to go out and "turn over an outhouse or dump a trash can in the filling station area." On Halloween, children in Fairplay and Alma would have competitions. "It wasn't destructive. It was just fun," she said.

For example, one year the Fairplay kids "went up there [to Alma] and pushed the Alma wagon. It was just a big old wagon that they had there in town." It was pushed in the river, she said. She said the Alma kids "would come down and tie bicycles to the flagpole, just little things like that."

Parties

Halloween wasn't only about kids creating mischief. There were parties of every type and for every age group. The parties, some of which included a dance, were held at various venues in Park County, and school parties, from elementary to high school, were reported in the *Flume*.

The society columns in Leadville and Aspen papers told about the Halloween parties of the well-to-do. In 1890, Delia Craddock, a 34-year-old unmarried Leadville woman originally from Ireland, "very pleasantly entertained a large circle of her young acquaintances . . . in true Halloween style" said the *Leadville Daily and Evening Chronicle* of November 3.

The party guests pulled taffy, ducked for apples, and danced, and they had an "elegant supper" about 11 p.m. The *Chronicle* gave a list of Craddock's high-society guests, which curiously did not include her future husband.

According to family history at www.ancestry.com, Craddock married in 1891 to a man with the last name of Murray, and by 1900, at age 44, she was a widow. That year she was listed as Delia Murray in the US Census and was living at the Convent of Mercy, St. Catherine's Home for Working Girls, near City Park in Denver with forty-one other women. It offered inexpensive room and board for single, employed women as well as night classes in cooking, dressmaking, needlework, music, painting, and sewing. The home closed soon after 1900, and Murray's trail runs cold at that point.

Myths and Games

Myths of Halloween focus on the ability to tell the future, and especially who one's future spouse would be, at least according to a story in the December 19, 1889, *Aspen Daily Chronicle*. Among the ways to find the identity of one's future wife or husband, it said, was to place a glass of water containing a small sliver of wood on a table near one's bed before retiring on Halloween.

"In the night you will dream of falling from a bridge into the river, and of being rescued by your future wife or husband, whom you will see as distinctly as though viewed with waking eyes," the story said.

Halloween parties also focused on one's future spouse. In a game that promised "great amusement," two hickory nuts were placed about three inches apart on the hearth in front of an open fire, said an 1897 edition of the monthly *Ladies Home Journal*. One represented the girl who placed it there; the other represented the one she wished to be her future spouse. If the nuts burned brightly, the two would have a happy marriage. If the nut placed for the man jumped toward the other nut, there would be a proposal before the next new moon, it said.

Trick or Treat

Trick-or-treating originated in the mid-1800s. That's when Americans first adopted a custom from Irish immigrants of dressing up in costumes and going from house to house asking for food or money. The custom gained popularity in the 1920s as an attempt to make the holiday more community-centered and less expensive—and to get away from the vandalism and pranks of earlier years.

1908 Halloween greeting card. *By The Rose Company [Public domain], via Wikimedia Commons.*

Halloween Spending

American society has come a long way from the expectation of a missing garden gate on Halloween night. Estimates vary from $6 billion to $8 billion spent annually in the United States on Halloween—including candy, pumpkins, decorations, and costumes—both for people and their pets. It's the country's second-largest commercial holiday, according to www.history.com. But that Halloween spending is still nowhere near what the United States spends on Christmas, the largest commercial holiday. Christmas decorations alone account for $6 billion in sales annually, and total annual spending is estimated at $465 billion, according to the ABC News website.

Chapter 16

Willia Hamilton Johnson

Alma Miner's Wife

In a small red diary, Willia Hamilton Johnson recorded her day-to-day life and innermost thoughts for five years, from January 1, 1920, to December 31, 1924. With space on the page for only a few lines a day, she captured the routine and the remarkable, and she inadvertently gave future generations a look at life in Alma's early years.

Willia and Bob Johnson on their wedding day, October 1, 1904. *Photo courtesy of Sharon Amos.*

She may have been an ordinary woman for her time, but Willia seems far from ordinary when compared to women of today. She was as much at home trapping animals for their fur as she was using her sewing machine. She mastered cake baking in Alma's two-mile-high altitude and enjoyed fishing at Antero Reservoir and Sacramento Creek. She went "Kodaking," which in 1920s slang meant taking photos, originally coined by those using a Kodak camera. Willia developed the film and printed her photos, and she was an author. A well-written booklet containing stories and poems about her life, *The Call of the Mines and Other Stories,* was published in 1974, when Willia was ninety years old.

She rarely worked outside the home, and she and her husband, Bob Johnson, moved often as he searched for work—in the mines, in an auto repair shop, and on a farm in southwestern Colorado. Bob much preferred working in mines, and he worked in some of Colorado's famous ones—the Tomboy near Telluride, the Climax in Lake County, and the May Day near Durango—as well as some of Alma's prominent mines—the North London, the South London, the Dolly Varden, and the Sweet Home.

Bob and Willia Johnson lived in this cabin near the London Mines in 1920. *From Willia's photo album, courtesy of Sharon Amos.*

On January 1, 1920, when Willia was thirty-six years old and Bob was forty-five, they lived in a one-room cabin at the gold-producing London Mines in Mosquito Gulch. It wasn't an easy life. Although the US economy boomed during the 1920s, the Johnsons weren't wealthy. Two weeks into the New Year, Bob was given notice from mine manager Charles Aicher that he would soon be laid off. When it happened two days later, Willia cried. She wondered if they would ever have a home of their own. She wrote that she didn't know what she and Bob would do or where they would go and that it was the "same old story"—the couple would have to move again.

At the London Mill in Mosquito Gulch, 1924. Willia, left, with friends Mrs. Blomquist (center) and Mrs. Brown. *From Willia's photo album, courtesy of Sharon Amos.*

They moved to the Singleton home in Alma for a few days and later to a rental home owned by the Weber family. They talked about moving away from Alma, and in the meantime Bob found temporary work cutting firewood. He also worked on the "flivver" (1920s slang for a small, inexpensive, old car that usually gave a rough ride) to try to get it running in case he couldn't find work and he and Willia had to move away.

Luckily, Bob did get the car running, and he also found work. He started at the Dolly Varden Mine on Mount Bross on February 1, 1920. The same day that Bob went to work up the hill, Willia probably could have used his help at home—she fell and sprained her wrist, nearly breaking it, and the stovepipe fell down.

Bob wasn't overly fond of the Dolly. He complained that the workers had to melt snow for all their personal water use as well as for water used in the mine. He complained that he was never outside, that he was always inside the house or working in the mine. But Bob stuck it out at the Dolly while Willia stayed home alone. It took several hours to walk or ride a horse to and from the mine, so Bob typically worked for a week at a time before he came home for a break. Their communication was through letters and the telephone.

While Bob was away, Willia kept busy. She was an accomplished fur trapper, and in her traps she caught a variety of the wildlife that roamed around Alma. Muskrats, badgers, rabbits, weasels, coyotes, and foxes were mentioned in the diary. Once she wrote about trapping "a fine mink" that earned her $15 (about $180 in 2015 dollars). She sewed an apron and mailed it to her mother as a birthday gift. She made many of her own clothes, including a gray silk dress, "surely a hard job as material was scarce," she wrote.

She rode horses, often to check animal traps, with a good friend whom she called Mrs. Sheldon in the diary and never once by her first name, Loura (or Lura). She also attended functions at the Ladies Aid Hall in Alma. When Bob was home, they got together with other couples and had dinner before playing cards or listening to the radio.

Bad and Good

Bob and Willia seemed to get along most of the time, but Willia mentioned days when Bob "ranted" about things she did, such as on April 2, 1923.

Bob came down from the mine, and Bill and Loura Sheldon and a man named John came over for dinner and to play cards. John was part of the reason for Bob and Willia's fight the next day.

Bob accused Willia of having company at their home all the time when he was away, and that the company was eating all of their food. He said she was seeing too much of their friend John, that she shouldn't have quit her job (as a cook at the Sweet Home Mine), and that if he couldn't have any fun (because he was working), Willia shouldn't either.

After the fight, Willia went to the store for milk. When she returned, Bob was gone. She fixed dinner "and waited and waited" for him. A neighbor later told her Bob took off on his horse headed back to the mine. Two days later Bob finally phoned Willia. After that argument, she wrote that "maybe there was to be no future with him" and that henceforth she would go day by day until something happened. But the marriage lasted. The two were together for more than fifty-four years—until Bob's death in 1959.

Bob Johnson, far right, next to Willia, with an unidentified other couple at the London Mines shack in the early 1920s. *From Willia's photo album, courtesy of Sharon Amos.*

There were good times too. Just a few days before the big fight, on March 27, Bob called from the mine and asked Willia to meet him. Willia borrowed a horse named Kit from Weber's livery and met Bob up on the mountain. She said she "enjoyed it so much."

Another time, Bob was working the day of his forty-ninth birthday on March 22, 1923. A day later he came home, and Willia had a cake ready for him. They attended a dance and bazaar at the "hall" (probably Alma's Ladies Aid Hall), and Bob went back up to the mine early the next morning.

Worst Fears Realized

Beginning about the first of April 1923, and lasting for several months, Willia did not feel well. Her stomach hurt, she was nauseous, and she had severe headaches. By June she was feeling worse. In an entry on June 1 she said she was "not well at all, just barely able to crawl around." And the next day it was worse: "I was so sick I thought I was going to die."

On June 5, her thirty-ninth birthday, Willia made a decision to call the doctor. On June 8, Bob and Willia went to see Dr. L. M. Gwinn in Fairplay. And that's the day Willia wrote in her diary, "My worst fears were all true."

She was pregnant. The doctor said he would take her to Salida the following Monday, June 11, for an operation to terminate the pregnancy. In anticipation of the trip to Salida, Willia said she was "so nervous all day, [she] could hardly do anything."

As it turned out, the doctor didn't take Willia to Salida. He called on Sunday to say the Salida doctor, George Curfman, would not operate until Willia consulted a specialist in Denver. Willia saw Dr. C. B. Ingraham in Denver on June 28.

Best Day of Life

Even though she was sick in the car traveling to the city, Willia felt well enough to see a show with Bob the evening before her appointment. It was *Enemies of Women*, a silent movie starring Lionel Barrymore. Willia said it was good. After seeing the doctor, Willia wrote in her diary, "In some ways (this is) the greatest day of my life—if doctors can be depended upon."

Willia wrote that Dr. Ingraham thought that she had a good chance "to go through with it this time." The choice of words indicates Willia may have miscarried in the past. The pregnancy was progressing, but Willia didn't feel well for more than a few days at a time for the entire pregnancy.

Bob and Willia moved to Salida in November 1923 to live with her mother. Bob worked at the silver-producing Rawley Mine west of Villa Grove in the town of Bonanza until the mine shut down later that month. Even with Bob out of work, the two were happy. She wrote about her joy in pregnancy in a summary of the year 1923: "The biggest surprise of all was when I learned that I was to become a mother after nearly 20 years of married life and after doctors had told me it was impossible. I expected (the) stork Dec. 20th, but the year passed and nothing happened."

The last entry for the year was that "1923 closed leaving us all looking forward to the biggest event of our lives, the coming of the stork, and hoping and praying that it may come speedily."

Worst Day

On January 7, 1924, Willia received a letter from her old friend Loura Sheldon, asking the question everyone back in Alma wanted to know, how Willia was doing. Perhaps Willia didn't answer her friend, but in her diary she wrote, "(I) haven't the heart to tell them."

On January 21, Dr. Curfman determined the baby was overdue. Willia met him the next day at midwife Kate Van Perryman's home. He induced labor, and on January 24, after three days of labor, Robert Lee Johnson was born. He gave a few gasps and died.

Later Years

Bob and Willia adopted their son, Charles, sometime between 1925, when he was born, and 1927, when the family moved to Ignacio, Colorado, near Durango, and started farming. A few years later, during the depression, the family was financially ruined.

In 1932, they were back in Alma, where Bob worked repairing small engines. In 1936, they were part of the congregation that built Alma's Stone Church. Willia's dream of owning a home of her own was finally realized when the Johnsons bought a home in Buena Vista in 1946.

Willia died in Salida in 1979 at age ninety-five and is buried next to Bob in Buena Vista's Mount Olivet Cemetery.

Books by Willia Hamilton Johnson. *Photo by the author.*

Note: Sources for this story include the unpublished diary of Willia Vance Hamilton Johnson, 1920–1924, available at the Park County Local History Archives, and "The Call of the Mines and Other Stories" by Willa (Willia) V. Johnson," copyright 1974. Special thanks go to Sharon Amos, great-grandniece of Willia Johnson, for filling in the blanks.

Chapter 17

South Park Game Preserve

1936 Plan to End Park County

There would be no Park County in Colorado today if a 1936 plan had gone through. All the land except for a few hundred thousand acres would have been converted into the South Park Game Preserve. The governor gave his approval; discovery of oil near Hartsel stopped it.

Headline, March 6, 1936, *Eagle Valley Enterprise*, Eagle County, Colorado. The headline seemed to overestimated the total number of acres, later articles gave estimates of about 1.3 million acres.
Clip courtesy of Colorado Historic Newspapers,
www.ColoradoHistoricNewspapers.org.

Propose to Turn Park County Into Big Game Preserve

GOVERNOR ENDORSES PLAN—SAYS REFUGE WOULD BE A GREAT ASSET TO STATE—TO EMBRACE MORE THAN 2,000,000 ACRES OF LAND.

On February 28, 1936, Governor Edwin C. Johnson first heard the proposal to turn nearly 1.3 million acres of Park County land into the South Park Game Preserve. Eight days later he gave his endorsement, saying the preserve would be a vital asset to Colorado.

Promoters said Park County would go back to its natural state before its lush pastures were overgrazed and its water was wasted on hayfield irrigation. A small sliver—157,000 acres along the county's northern boundary, between Fairplay and Estabrook—was to be spared from the preserve and absorbed into nearby counties. Mining claims would be the only private property within the preserve. The rest of the county, about 630,000 acres of private, federal, state, and county-owned land and 644,000 acres of the Pike National Forest, would become the South Park Game Preserve.

View of South Park from Davis Overlook on Boreas Pass. *Photo by the author.*

Park County would have ceased to exist had the plan been finalized. Its land would have belonged to no county, and its inhabitants would have been encouraged to sell out and move away. The region would have been overrun with up to 60,000 head of imported big game animals and hundreds of thousands of fish, birds, and smaller animals. The region was slated to have become a paradise for hunters, anglers, and recreationists and a huge tourist attraction, billed as the largest of its kind in the United States.

Once its residents heard the details of the plan, they would be pleased, said a story in the March 27, 1936, *Park County Republican and Fairplay Flume.* The opinion was attributed to county commissioner Harry Bishop. In a later edition, he said the county government would not oppose the plan, and he believed there would be very little opposition from its residents. But Bishop's comments were made before he had talked to his constituents, who, not surprisingly, did have opposition to selling out their homes and livelihood to the government.

But in the end, it didn't matter that residents weren't consulted by the commissioner or the governor. In the end, preservation of the land in pristine condition didn't matter either, because in April 1936, oil was discovered north of Hartsel, near today's James Mark Jones State Wildlife Area. The well was reported to be a gusher, and that discovery put the game preserve plans on hold while oil exploration continued.

"Naturally, if there is an oil field there, we must either abandon the game preserve plan or change it considerably," said Edward D. Foster, state planning commission director, in a story in the April 24, 1936, *Steamboat (Springs) Pilot.* "We can do nothing but wait until the extent of the discovery is determined."

The article didn't mention why the game preserve plan should "naturally" be abandoned or changed, but it was implied that even though the purpose of the game preserve was to conserve water; to preserve the beauty of the area; to provide a sanctuary for animals, birds and fish; and to become a haven of recreation for the entire United States, the plan couldn't hold a candle to the huge monetary profits the oil discovery promised.

In 1936, newspapers were filled with the activities of Adolph Hitler as World War II loomed on the horizon. And the country was in the grip of the Great Depression, which lasted until 1939. The "promise of one of the most important developments in the petroleum industry of Colorado ever reported," as the discovery was called in the April 17, 1936, *Republican,* was welcome news throughout the state. It was envisioned that both Hartsel and Fairplay would grow tremendously by the predicted windfall of 10,000 barrels of oil per day.

(For most of their history, the shortened name of the merged newspapers, the *Park County Republican* and *Fairplay Flume,* was the *Flume.* In this chapter, as it was in 1936, the short name is the *Republican.*)

Plan Presenters

It wasn't a fly-by-night plan presented to Governor Johnson. Respected representatives of the US Biological Survey (now US Fish and Wildlife), the Colorado State Conservation Council (state affiliate to the National Wildlife Federation), and Park County's own Kenneth W. Chalmers, state coordinator of the Soil Conservation Service (now Natural Resources Conservation Service), approached the governor.

Chalmers was born in Colorado Springs in 1899 and lived in South Park as early as 1905 at the age of six. He left the county to attend high school at the Episcopalian College in Salina, Kansas, and continued his education at Colorado A & M in Fort Collins (now Colorado State University), where he was on the debate team, worked on the yearbook staff, and was a member of Alpha Zeta fraternity (an organization for students in agriculture and natural resources fields). A World War I draft notice interrupted college, but Chalmers returned to Fort Collins after the war to earn a degree in animal husbandry in 1922.

After his college graduation, Chalmers lived in Park County at the EM Ranch (called the Santa Maria Ranch in 2016) near Hartsel. He served on the boards of the Park County Wool Growers Association, the Leadville Holy Cross Wool Growers Association, and the Colorado Wool Growers Association. His career at the Soil Conservation Service began in 1935. He worked there for 27 years, leaving in March 1962 due to ill health. He died a month later and is buried at Denver's Fairmount Cemetery.

Plan Explanation

Residents of Park County gathered to discuss the plan with Chalmers at a March 28, 1936, Lions Club meeting in the Fairplay Hotel. Attendees were representative of some of the county's most recognized families, including Teter, Witcher, Crouch, Buyer, Hand, and Singleton. The *Republican* editor, John Leuthold, was there and wrote a front-page story about the meeting, where Chalmers was introduced as the man most familiar with the pending game preserve.

Chalmers said that dryland homesteading in Park County, and especially South Park, was a complete failure. It destroyed the natural range, and too much water was used to irrigate hay. He said South Park water would be better used if it was allowed to flow downstream to other locales where the earning potential of the water would be half a million dollars more per year.

Chalmers's enthusiastic talk focused on money, specifically how much the county could save by eliminating certain services that would no longer be needed, such as the county's eleven schools, maintenance on roads, and most of the county government. He talked about the considerable earning potential there was in surcharging the cost of hunting in the new game preserve and charging a

25 percent fee on profits from beaver pelts. He said the county would reap increased taxes and fees from hotels, summer homes, and dude ranches.

In fact, he spent considerable time emphasizing increased revenue and decreased costs for Park County, when, according to the plan, there would be no Park County. Residents would be encouraged to sell their land and move away, although, Chalmers said, nobody would be forced to sell. He mentioned tracts of privately held land within national forests and said private land within the game preserve would be handled in the same way.

Chalmers had an answer for just about every contingency that members of the audience brought up. When a spectator questioned how 15,000 head of big game could be shot in one hunting season, Chalmers said perhaps hunting would be allowed year round. But neither Chalmers nor anyone else involved in the plan anticipated the discovery of oil in South Park.

Pronghorn in South Park, March 2013. *Photo by the author.*

Oil and Gas

The South Park Oil Company had been drilling at a site northwest of Hartsel for nearly two years when news broke in April 1936 that oil was struck at four thousand feet below the surface. Within a few days "excited onlookers from Fairplay and Alma . . . even from Denver" were on the scene, said the April 17, 1936, *Steamboat Pilot.*

The *Republican*'s headline covered the full width of its April 17 edition: "South Park's Oil Fountain is a Gusher," and above the masthead, "Oil not only quiets troubled waters, but has just demonstrated that it can also put a quietus on a fool game-refuge scheme." It was evident the editor thought little of the South Park Game Preserve.

As the months flew by, nothing but good news came from the drill site dubbed State No. 1. Oil gushed at a thousand barrels a day. It was predicted that daily production would soon be 10,000 barrels. Natural gas was present, coming out of the well with a "deafening hiss and roar" when uncapped. Plans were to immediately sink four more wells on the 2,700-acre site.

Derricks of South Park Oil Company circa 1930s. *Park County Local History Archives, source: Clint Eshe.*

Presumably it would be great news for the narrow gauge Colorado & Southern Railroad (successor of the Denver, South Park & Pacific). The nearest track to the oil wells was five miles west at Garo. The convenience of the track in transporting oil may have been all the incentive the failing railroad needed to stay alive. But as it happened, rail traffic was discontinued in April 1937, about a year after the pipe dream of South Park oil riches died.

The *Republican* never reported that the wells were declining, but the stories were shorter with every edition; sometimes weeks would go by with no mention of the Hartsel oil. A search of the *Republican* issues through the middle of 1937 indicated that the last mention of the wells was on September 18, 1936, when the State No. 1 well was down to 5,000 feet and was pulling up "considerable lime and sand with oil saturation." A second well had some trouble with "infirm ground," but drilling was proceeding, and the shaft was down to 1,000 feet.

The End and The Future

Even as the oil wells were not mentioned again in the *Republican,* neither was the game preserve. After almost seven months of ups and downs and an uncertain future for residents and property owners of Park County, the year 1936 ended with the status quo preserved. There was no longer any threat of losing land to the game preserve or of enduring the noise and resource damage from drilling.

As for the future, State No. 1 was just one of the twenty-three oil wells drilled in South Park between 1893 and 1970 that failed to produce in the long-term; the few wells drilled after 1970 were equally unsuccessful. Depending on a decision that the Bureau of Land Management, or BLM, makes as early as 2016, drilling may be denied in the area for the following two decades.

In mid-2015, the BLM invited public comment and opinions on future oil and gas drilling leases in South Park. Results from that survey and other criteria have been planned for use in a BLM decision about when, where, or if drilling leases would be allowed in South Park for the following twenty years. (The decision had not been made before this book went to press in mid-2016.)

Coincidently, the major arguments offered by the public in 2015 against oil and gas drilling are eerily familiar: to protect South Park's pristine environment and wildlife; to preserve its hunting, fishing, and recreation opportunities and continue the benefits of the money they bring to the county; and to keep its rivers and reservoirs pure for their use downstream as drinking water for Denver and Colorado Springs.

The reasons sound somewhat like the motives behind the "fool game-refuge scheme."

1960s–1970s

Chapter 18

Autumn 1963

County Reacts to JFK Assassination; Local News Headlines

Park County and the nation were getting ready for Thanksgiving and Christmas in 1963 when the news of President John F. Kennedy's assassination reached every corner of the country and most parts of the world. Kennedy was shot at about 12:30 p.m. on Friday, November 22, 1963, as he rode in a motorcade through downtown Dallas. It was six days before the November 28 Thanksgiving holiday.

In local news in the autumn of 1963, phones were updated to dial-up service, theft of copper wire happened practically under the nose of Sheriff Joe Hurst, South Park lost its homecoming game, and school enrollment figures were reported.

Kennedy

In Park County, news of the president's death was received just as the students at South Park High School were served lunch. The *Flume* of November 28 reported that few students were interested in eating after hearing the news.

Throughout the county, meetings were canceled or postponed, and most workplaces were closed, including schools; county, state, and federal offices; and the bank.

President Lyndon Johnson declared a day of mourning on Monday, November 25, the day of Kennedy's funeral in Washington, D.C., and burial at Arlington National Cemetery. Park County churches also held memorial services, including the South Park Community Church (Sheldon Jackson Chapel) in Fairplay and the Platte Canyon Community Church in Bailey, where about 100 people attended.

During the Bailey service, the congregation sang "America" and "America the Beautiful." A requiem mass (mass for someone who has died) was held at St. Joseph's Catholic Church in Fairplay, where Father McInerney's sermon was "How to be a Good American."

News of the assassination was mentioned on every nearly page of the November 28, 1963, *Flume*. The columnist for Bailey and Platte Canyon, Alice Wonder, was the most expressive in her opinion:

> Never in all the years have I been called upon to tell of so sad and tragic an act as it is [my] unhappy duty to tell of this week. The world will long remember the fiendish, dastardly assassination of our young President Kennedy in Dallas, Texas, by a creature who can not be classed as a human being (Oswald) who was in turn slain by another assassin. It is useless to try to tell of the shock, sorrow and grief that has encompassed our nation.

The Republican Women of Park County canceled a Christmas party and postponed a meeting in observance of a thirty-day moratorium on public meetings, speeches, and political activity called for by the Republican National Committee, said the December 5, 1963, *Flume*. The Park County Jane Jefferson Club (a nationwide club, named after Thomas Jefferson's mother, that was established in 1902 for women who wanted to be more involved in the Democratic Party) had previously scheduled a Christmas party for December 11. The party was canceled, and instead the club held a memorial service on that date.

Assassination

Kennedy, elected in 1960, had not announced his candidacy for the 1964 election, but he was preparing to run, according to information from the Boston-based John F. Kennedy Presidential Library and Museum. On November 21,

1963, the president and First Lady Jacqueline Kennedy left for a two-day, five-city tour of Texas. Kennedy had campaigned in eleven states since September, but it was Mrs. Kennedy's first extended public appearance since the couple's two-day-old son, Patrick Bouvier Kennedy, had died in August of infant respiratory distress syndrome.

Head table at the Fort Worth Chamber of Commerce breakfast, Hotel Texas, Fort Worth, Texas, November 22, 1963. (L-R) Lady Bird Johnson, Vice President Lyndon B. Johnson, First Lady Jacqueline Kennedy, and President John F. Kennedy. (Unidentified man in background.) *Public domain photo by Cecil Stoughton, White House Photographs, John F. Kennedy Presidential Library and Museum, Boston.*

After visiting San Antonio and Houston on November 21, the presidential entourage continued to Fort Worth on November 22, where the president spoke at a chamber of commerce breakfast. Afterward, the group took a thirteen-minute flight to Dallas, where Kennedy was scheduled to speak at a luncheon at the Dallas Trade Mart.

At 12:30 p.m., as the Kennedys rode in an open convertible limousine from the airport through downtown Dallas, gunfire erupted from the Texas School Book Depository. The president was struck in the neck and head, and he slumped, bleeding, over his wife. The limousine sped to Parkland Memorial Hospital, only minutes away, but nothing could be done to save the president. A Catholic priest was summoned; Kennedy was given last rites and was pronounced dead at one o'clock.

In 1963, *Flume* columns continued to report on cancellations and memorial services for three weeks after the assassination, but other events made the news as well.

Lyndon Baines Johnson takes the oath of office aboard Air Force One at Love Field, Dallas, Texas, on November 22, 1963. *Public domain photo by Cecil Stoughton, White House Photographs, John. F. Kennedy Presidential Library and Museum, Boston.*

Dial-Up

In telephone technology, Park County was forty years behind Denver, where dial-up phones were in use in the 1920s, and nine years behind Boulder's dial-up service, which began in 1954. But at midnight on Saturday, December 14, 1963, Park County was ready for the change. Mountain States Telephone & Telegraph, or MST&T, flipped a switch, and the county moved from two-digit phone numbers connected with the assistance of an operator to the still-used seven-digit 836 (South Park) and 838 (Platte Canyon) exchanges.

And seemingly overnight the "Hello Girls" were gone.

"Hello Girls," (a term used in the December 12, 1963, *Flume*) was the typical name for women who said "hello" when one rang the switchboard in the days before direct telephone dialing. It was first used to describe women switchboard operators in the US Army Signal Corps during World War I, according to www.worldwar1.com.

No longer could area residents "contact some person merely by asking the operator to call the nearest home," the *Flume* of December 12, 1963, said. And if one wanted "information of any kind," the story continued, "those Denver operators just aren't going to be of much help to you."

In a final word about the "Hello Girls," the *Flume* of December 12, 1963, said it spoke for the community in saying the departing Park County telephone operators were sincerely appreciated. "We are sure that this friendly service will not soon be forgotten by the great majority."

Vintage 1960s rotary dial telephone formerly owned by Fairplay teacher and elementary school namesake Edith Teter. *Photo by the author.*

Crime Solved

One week after the telephone change, crime made the front page of the December 19, 1963, *Flume.* It was a story about the theft of copper wire from the South Platte Dredging Company near Fairplay. Sheriff Hurst had his officers watching the site each night "with no sign ever of the thieves," the story said.

The theft was solved when two deputies and the sheriff were visiting with some local residents in the Sheriff's Office. A man named Jim Settele came in to see the sheriff, and soon after another person came into the office. While making small talk, the second visitor asked how the case of the copper theft was coming along. Hurst answered that there were not any good leads, at which time Settele inquired who it was that "was rolling up copper just then at the dredging property."

The officers rushed out of the office and caught three Denver men loading copper into a car. The men were arrested and taken to court for arraignment on December 12. None could post the $10,000 bond set for each, and all three were taken to the Chaffee County Jail. The *Flume* story said that after catching the thieves in daylight, Hurst and his deputies "are now wondering if the thefts have been taking place in daylight all of the time, as the property has been watched very closely at night for a long time."

South Platte Dredge near Fairplay. *Park County Local History Archives, Sanborn postcard, South Park Historical Foundation.*

Homecoming

South Park High School played its homecoming football game on Saturday, October 19, 1963, and, according to the October 24, 1963, *Flume*, "events went off smoothly except for the football score." But it wasn't so bad. "The team came closest to winning of any game this year," the *Flume* story said. The final was Westcliffe 13, South Park 6.

The festivities began on Friday night, when students met at the school at seven o'clock and "snake danced" over to the 4-H barn for a bonfire and pep rally. On Saturday morning, the elementary and high school bands, accompanied by twirlers for "color and interest," marched through downtown Fairplay.

In the week before the big game, the football team voted by secret ballot for homecoming queen and two princesses. At halftime on the field, Charlotte Ansley, a senior, was crowned queen by the football team captain, Doug Leaf.

Elected princesses were senior Barbara Kintz and junior Melissa McFarland, who were escorted by football players John Dickerson and Mike McNamara.

School Enrollment

In 1963 the total enrollment in Park County schools was 295 students; of those, fifty-three percent, or 155, attended schools in the South Park district and forty-seven percent, or 140, attended schools in the Platte Canyon district, according to the September 5, 1963, *Flume.*

In 2013, when this part of the book was written, total enrollment in Park County was 1,621 students. Sixty-four percent, or 1,031, attended Platte Canyon schools and thirty-six percent, or 590 students, attended South Park schools, reported the November 22, 2013, *Flume.*

Chapter 19

Ed Snell Memorial Run

And Its Bar-Bet Beginning

There are certain events in life that, in retrospect, are the game changers. If Bill Reeves and Tom Knebel had not gone to the bar that night (Fairplay's no-longer-existing J-Bar-J), if the conversation had not drifted to their high school track records, and if their drinking buddies had not encouraged the wager, then the fund-raising Ed Snell Memorial Run might never have developed. Its charity funds might never have been raised, and its beneficial life-changing assistance might never have been given.

But the stars lined up that night, and the Ed Snell Memorial Run was born. Many lives have changed for the better all because two local construction workers bet a beer on who would win a six-mile race from Fairplay to Alma on a cold February night in 1979.

Bill Reeves (left) and Tom Knebel meet again in Fairplay, in August 2014, thirty-six years after the first race. *Photo by the author.*

Bill Reeves tells it this way:

> One evening, after a few brewskis, the topic of conversation came around to high school track, with both of us recalling how great we were at long distance. Of course, as time went on and the beer kept flowing, our times kept getting better. With encouragement from our friends, it was decided the only way to resolve the dispute was to have a foot race between the two of us. The race would start at the Park Bar in Fairplay and end in Alma at the AOB [Alma's Only Bar]. The stakes would be a beer to the winner.

The two chose a day the following week to race. Both showed up in their work clothes—jeans, heavy coats, and work boots. After a quick beer and cheers from the bar patrons, the two set out in the cold, dark night for the AOB. Reeves won and said, "I'm still savoring that beer."

The Reeves/Knebel race from Fairplay to Alma didn't have a name and wasn't planned to continue past that first race. It was simply Knebel and Reeves running to determine who would buy beers in Alma. Ultimately it was the onset of an annual event created to raise money for South Park residents in need.

Ed Snell Memorial Fund

The first fund bearing Ed Snell's name was set up in 1978, seven months before the Reeves/Knebel wager, when Knebel ran in Fairplay's annual World Championship Pack Burro Race. His sponsor was the *Park County Republican and Fairplay Flume* through its then owner and publisher, Richard Hamilton. Knebel said Hamilton suggested he use his entry in the burro race as a way to generate funds for two local families that had suffered tragedies the previous year.

Knebel and his burro didn't come close to finishing that race, or, as he tells it, "I fell at the starting line and limped along for about twenty-five miles [the burro race is 29 miles] when my burro kneeled down as we were approaching Park City on our return to town. The race officials, in their eagerness to call it a day, yanked us out of the race."

Knebel did, however, collect approximately $1,000 in donations. The money was divided and deposited anonymously into the bank accounts of the two families.

Namesake

It was Hamilton's idea to name the fund after Ed Snell. His reasoning was that when he and Snell worked together to bring a health department to Park County, Hamilton observed Snell—who was on the county planning commission at the time—to be a "grand human being and a miner who cared about the environment."

Ed Snell (1904–1975) was a man who "never lost faith in mankind. He took people in who needed help," said Alma resident Erik Swanson in talking about his Uncle Ed. He said Snell helped those who needed financial help or needed to get their life back on track after living on the streets. He gave them jobs in Alma-area mines, provided them with a place to sleep, and helped them get rehabilitated.

Ed Snell "was chosen to be immortalized because of his giving spirit," said Swanson's wife, Beth Swanson. And that is what the race stands for today. Funds have been used for, among other things, a liver transplant; expenses of a terminally ill patient and her family; and medical, dental, and vision bills. Participants pay a fee to run or walk the paved trail from Fairplay (at 9,953 feet above sea level) to Alma (at 10,586 feet), and are also encouraged to collect outside donations for the cause. As the race became more popular over the years, the official distance was increased to 10K, or 6.21 miles.

Edward Louis Snell, age sixty-eight, in 1972. *Photo from the personal collection of Erik C. Swanson.*

1981 Race

The first race bearing the Ed Snell name was in February 1981.

The scene was nearly the same; Knebel was in the J-Bar-J when another friend, Don Long, challenged him to the same race that Knebel and Reeves had run two years earlier. Hamilton was present that night (although his recollection is that it was at the Fairplay Hotel bar) and recalls that Long said something to the effect that even after smoking cigarettes and drinking beer, he could beat Knebel in a race to Alma.

Hamilton figured the race between Long and Knebel was a way to revive the Ed Snell Memorial Fund. So the race was advertised in the *Flume* and, although Long and Knebel were the only two runners, the race generated $490 in donations from local businesses and individuals and was called the "First Annual Ed Snell Memorial Fund Foot Race."

Knebel tied his record from the previous race, which was good enough to win. Long attributed his loss to the wind that was aggravating a toothache and the fact that he was running at a higher altitude, being three inches taller than Knebel, according to the February 19, 1981, *Flume*.

A year later, in 1982, the race attracted about twenty runners, and has grown slightly over time to thirty-one runners in 2015.

Celebrity Runners

Local and regional runners typically participate in the Ed Snell Memorial Run, but for a period of time in the mid-to-late 1990s, a few celebrity runners showed up for the race. Although Federico Peña and his wife, Ellen Hart Peña, could have been considered locals because they owned property in the county, they were better known for their activities outside Park County. Ellen Hart Peña—lawyer, world class runner, Ironman Triathlon competitor, and, since 2008, a member of the Colorado Running Hall of Fame—ran the Ed Snell race more than once in the 1990s. In the years she ran in the Park County race, she was married to Federico Peña, a former mayor of Denver (1983-1991) and at the time the US Secretary of Transportation under President Bill Clinton (1993-1997).

Reeves said that one year, Hart Peña "finished the race in Alma in record time, and ran back to Fairplay to get her car, shouting encouragement to the runners along the way." (Traditionally entrants park in Alma and are shuttled to Fairplay where the race starts.) "One year, she brought along her friend, Frank Shorter," Reeves continued.

Shorter won a gold medal in the marathon at the 1972 Summer Olympics in Munich, Germany, where he was born. He later lived in Boulder, Colorado, and was "a driving force in the distance running boom that started in the United States in the late 1970s," according to *USA Track and Field*. He is a member of several halls of fame, including those of Colorado Sports, Colorado Running, USA Track & Field, Honolulu, and US Olympic athletes.

Tom Knebel (left) and Ellen Hart Peña before an Ed Snell Memorial Run in the 1990s. *Photo courtesy of Kathy Reeves.*

Knebel was thrilled to be running with Hart Peña and Shorter.

"I was standing next to Frank [Shorter] at the starting line when Ellen [Hart Peña]—though she forgot my name—pointed me out to Frank as being the race founder. By the time the starting gun was fired, I was so pumped up that I sprinted for the first quarter of a mile and led both Frank and Ellen and all others for that distance. They soon passed me as if I was standing still, as that is exactly what I was doing, for I was ready to pass out from exhaustion. I walked most of the rest of the race, but I can say that I once outran those two Olympic stars."

Snell History

The history of Ed Snell in Park County dates back 100 years before the Knebel and Reeves wager, to 1879. It was then that the first Ed Snell, Edward Daniel Snell, arrived in Alma from Wyoming as an eight-year-old boy. He was the father of the race's namesake and was born in Sherman, Wyoming (now a ghost town), on April 19, 1871. He moved to Cheyenne, Wyoming, in 1878 and to Alma a year later. His parents had interests in mining claims in Buckskin Gulch as early as 1880, including the Silver Wave, the US Mint, and the Golden Queen.

The older Ed Snell married Johannah Hoffman in 1902. She was from a pioneer Alma-area family that ranched north of Alma at Dudley. Ed and Johannah had six children—Ida May, born in 1903, who died of meningitis at age 3; Edward Louis, born in 1904; Walter, born in 1906, who was murdered in Salida, Colorado, in 1943 at age 37; Eveitte, born in 1907, who married Glen Swanson and had their son, Erik; Norman, born in 1910, who was a recipient of the bronze Medal of Honor and the Purple Heart for his military service during World War II; and Clyde, another Alma-area Snell family miner.

Edward Daniel Snell owned a jack train (a string of burros used to haul supplies). He hauled groceries and supplies to the mines around Alma and hauled gold and silver ore back to town. He died at age forty-six on April 16, 1917. The cause of death was dropsy, today called congestive heart failure.

The family had witnessed the decline of their patriarch in the two years before his death as his heart gradually weakened. During that time, the elder Snell had sought healing at the Clark Magnetic Mineral Spring in Pueblo, Colorado. In a 1903 advertisement, it publicized its "national reputation for curing Bright's disease of the kidneys, rheumatism, diseases of the stomach, liver, blood, skin and urinary tract."

Although he also sought healing in Kingman, Arizona, and Loma Linda, California, the older Ed Snell started selling property he owned in Alma in 1915. The advertisement in the March 15, 1915, *Flume* said, "For sale cheap — 55 pack jacks and saddles, also 2 saddle horses." By February 1917, the pack string was down to thirty-five; the last advertisement for the jacks, placed by Mrs. Ed Snell, appeared in the May 11, 1917, *Flume*.

At his father's death, Edward Louis Snell was thirteen years old and the eldest surviving child. He continued with his schooling but missed a lot of days in caring for the burros until they were sold and in helping his mother with household duties, said Erik Swanson. The family raised chickens and owned a cow, but the majority of their meat was rabbit, hunted in the Alma area by the Snell brothers.

After her husband's death, Johannah Snell was on her own; there was no government help for a widow with five children. She took in laundry, was a cook at the mines, and moved her family to the Fairplay poorhouse. Ten-year-old Eveitte left school to help her mother with laundry and cooking.

Edward Louis Snell

The race namesake, Edward Louis Snell, was a miner and an ecologist and was an early day recycler, said Swanson. "Uncle Ed could always use something twice." But Snell wasn't just a miner; he had the skills of a geologist without having obtained the formal education, according to Swanson. Snell always had a collection of mineral specimens in his pockets. Swanson's memories from when he was a young boy included his Uncle Ed's always knowing where each specimen was found and what kind of mineral it was.

Edward Louis Snell, circa 1935.
Photo from the personal collection of Erik C. Swanson.

Students at the Colorado School of Mines in Golden visited Ed Snell at his mines yearly, and the pupils "never could believe that he wasn't a graduate of (Colorado School of) Mines. He knew more about (mining) than the professors," said Swanson.

Death

Edward Louis Snell died in nephew Erik Swanson's arms.

It was on February 19, 1975, in the Snell home on Fairplay's Front Street. That home in 2016 is occupied by the Fairplay Therapy Center. Snell thought he had the flu and was too ill to get his mail. Swanson went to the post office while his uncle put on a kettle of water for tea. While Swanson was gone, Snell passed out and fell to the floor. Swanson returned from the errand, saw his uncle on the floor, and raised his Uncle Ed's head. And then Snell died. He was two months short of his seventy-first birthday.

Ed Snell is buried in the Fairplay Cemetery near the grave of his maternal grandfather, Johannes Hoffman.

Bibliography

Books

American Philosophical Society. *Proceedings of the American Philosophical Society Held at Philadelphia for Promoting Useful Knowledge.* Vol. 29. Original 1891. London: Forgotten Books, 2013.

Barnosky, Anthony D. *Biodiversity Response to Climate Change in the Middle Pleistocene: The Porcupine Cave Fauna from Colorado.* London: University of California Press, 2004.

Browne, Edward Frederick. *The Silver Dollar: A Business View.* Denver: Chain & Hardy Company, 1892.

Colorado General Assembly. *Official Souvenir and Manual of the Fifteenth General Assembly of the State of Colorado.* Denver: E. J. Miller, 1905.

Comstock, Charles W. *Fifteenth Biennial Report of the State Engineer to the Governor of Colorado.* Denver: Smith-Brooks Printing Company, 1911.

Dyer, J. L. *The Snow-Shoe Itinerant: An Autobiography of Rev. John L. Dyer.* Cincinnati: Cranston & Stowe, 1889.

Geary, Edward A. *A History of Emery County.* Salt Lake City: Utah State Historical Society, 1996.

Jensen, Naomi Asay Anderson, Ada Valoy Cox, and Heather J. Miller. *Recollections and Snapshots: A Historical Sketch of Castle Dale.* Castle Dale, UT: Castle Dale First Ward, 1997.

Johnson, Willa V. *The Call of the Mines and Other Stories.* Gunnison, CO: self-published, 1974.

Johnson, Willia Hamilton. "Personal Diary 1920–1924" (unpublished manuscript, last modified December 31, 1924), Handwritten book.

Noel, Thomas J. *Colorado Catholicism: The Archdiocese of Denver 1857–1989.* Niwot, CO: University Press of Colorado, 1989.

Stone, Wilbur Fisk. *History of Colorado*. Vol. 4. Chicago: S. J. Clarke
    Publishing Company, 1918.
Supreme Court Justices, states of AZ, CA, CO, ID, KS, MT, NV, NM, OK,
    OR, UT, WA, WY. *The Pacific Reporter*. Vol. 194. January 31–February
    28, 1921. St. Paul, MN: West Publishing Company, 1921.
Twain, Mark (Samuel L. Clemens). *Roughing It*. Hartford, CT: American
    Publishing Company, 1872.

Documents

Brantigan, Charles O., and Nathan Zeschin. *The 1887 Denver Directory*. Vol.
    1. Denver: Canzona Publications, 2002.
California Death Index, 1905-1939.
Certificate of Registration of American Citizen, (T. C. Link). Mazatlán,
    Mexico, February 4, 1912.
Colorado Census, 1885.
Colorado State Business Directory, 1881. House of Representatives, 36.
Colorado State Parks. Castlewood Canyon State Park, The Castlewood Dam.
Colorado State University Yearbooks, 1921 and 1922.
Cory, Harry T., Dabney H. Maury and Herbert S. Crocker. *Report of
    Engineering Board of Review to Board of Water Commissioners*. Denver,
    August 15, 1922.
Denver Board of Water Commissioners. *Water for Tomorrow—The History,
    Results, Projections and Update of the Integrated Resource Plan*, February
    2002.
Denver Water. High Line Canal Trail Map, 2011.
Fisk, Charles C. *The Metro Denver Water Story—A Memoir*, 2005.
Mehls, Steven F. *Highline Extension Canal (Doherty Ditch)*. Historic
    American Engineering Record, Rocky Mountain Regional Office, National
    Park Service, US Department of the Interior, March 1992.
Miller, George Geoffrey. *The Link History, A Colorado Pioneer Family*.
    Appendix 09, Link Family History Documents, undated.
National Register of Historic Places. *Denver International Airport Historic
    Resources*, March 1992.
National Register of Historic Places, Inventory-Nomination Form. *Como
    Roundhouse, Railroad Depot and Hotel Complex*, April 1983.

Record of an Inquisition held on the body of deceased at King, Colorado, January 12, 1893.

Report of the Death of an American Citizen (James Andrew Link). American Consular Service, Guatemala City, Guatemala, February 15, 1913.

US Census: 1860, 1870, 1880, 1900, 1910, 1920, 1930, 1940.

US Supreme Court Records and Briefs: October term, 1898, No. 146.

Verdict of Jury at a Coroner's Inquest at King, Colorado, January 12, 1893.

Wandry, Craig J., Charles E. Barker and Richard M. Pollastro. *Park Basins Province (038)*. Undated.

Whitehorn, W. Clark. *Aspen and the Railroads*. Aspen, CO: Aspen Historical Society, 1993.

Wilson, M. Patrick, Colorado Bar Association. *Eminent Domain Law in Colorado*, September 2006.

Worley, John F. El Paso (Texas) Directory, 1907.

Periodicals

Barry, John M. "The site of origin of the 1918 influenza pandemic and its public health implications." *Journal of Translational Medicine*, January 20, 2004.

Bohning, Larry. "Wilbur Fisk Stone." *The Colorado Lawyer*, Official Publication of the Colorado Bar Association, July 2002.

Chandler, Allison. "The Story of Como & King Park, Colorado." *Denver Westerners Monthly Roundup*, February 1963.

Fetter, Rosemary. "Colorado History—Cherry Hills Village and Greenwood Village: Twin cities with different destinies." *Colorado Gambler*, May 21, 2014.

Gardiner, Harvey N. "Colorado's longest aerial tramway was at Leavick." Letter to the Editor, *Colorado Central Magazine*, January 2002.

Garrett, Thomas A. "Pandemic Economics: The 1918 Influenza and Its Modern-Day Implications." *Federal Reserve Bank of St. Louis Review*, March/April 2008.

Hansen, Doug. "Stagecoach expert tells of drivers, demands, dangers." *Cowboys and Indians*, July 2009.

Helmich, Mary A. "Stage styles—Not all were coaches!" Interpretation & Education Division, California State Parks, 2008.

Minke, Gary. "The coal mines of South Park." *Colorado Central Magazine,* October 2005.

Price, Charles F. "The Rampage of the Espinosas." *Colorado Central Magazine,* Part 1, October 2008. Part 2, November 2008.

Sanburn, Josh. "More Americans Planning to Spend Money on Halloween— And Pet Costumes—This Year." *Time,* September 26, 2012.

Newspapers—Contemporary Editions

Associated Press. "Antero Dam gets safety upgrade," *Denver Post,* August 19, 2013.

Ballard, Misi. "To my South Park neighbors," *Park County Republican & Fairplay Flume,* July 24, 2015.

Davidson, Dale. "Perley Wason, business pioneer," *Cortez Journal,* November 3, 2012.

Handy, Ryan Maye. "Oil and gas exploration near South Park concerns some in Colorado Springs area," *Gazette,* September 12, 2015.

Newspapers—Historic Editions

Aspen Daily Chronicle, Aspen, Colorado

Aspen Daily Times, Aspen, Colorado

Balfour News, Balfour, Colorado

Buena Vista Herald, Buena Vista, Colorado

Chaffee County Republican, Buena Vista, Colorado

Colorado Democrat, Buena Vista, Colorado

Colorado Mountaineer, Colorado Springs, Colorado

Colorado Transcript, Golden, Colorado

Colorado Chieftain, Pueblo, Colorado

Daily Camera, Boulder, Colorado

Daily Mining Journal, Black Hawk, Colorado

Daily Mining Record, Denver, Colorado

Daily News, Denver, Colorado

Deseret Evening News, Salt Lake City, Utah

Douglas County News, Castle Rock, Colorado

Eastern Utah Advocate, Price, Utah
El Paso Daily Times, El Paso, Texas
Emery County Progress, Castle Dale, Utah
Ephraim Enterprise, Ephraim, Utah
Fairplay Flume, Fairplay, Colorado
Fort Collins Courier, Fort Collins, Colorado
Greeley Tribune, Greeley, Colorado
Leadville Daily and Evening Chronicle, Leadville, Colorado
Leadville Herald Democrat, Leadville, Colorado
Park County Bulletin, Alma, Colorado
Park County Republican & Fairplay Flume, Fairplay, Colorado
Record-Journal of Douglas County, Castle Rock, Colorado
Rocky Mountain News, Denver, Colorado
Rocky Mountain Sun, Aspen, Colorado
Routt County Republican, Hayden, Colorado
Salt Lake Tribune, Salt Lake City, Utah
San Antonio Daily Express, San Antonio, Texas
San Bernardino County Sun, San Bernardino, California
Silver Cliff Rustler, Silver Cliff, Colorado
Spartanburg Herald, Spartanburg, South Carolina
Steamboat Pilot, Steamboat Springs, Colorado

Websites

"1906 Food and Drugs Act and Its Enforcement." http://www.fda.gov/About FDA/WhatWeDo/History/Origin/ucm054819.htm.
"Airline squeeze: It's not you, 'it's the seat.'" www.cnn.com/2012/05/30/travel/airline-seats/.
www.Ancestry.com: Public Member Trees for Louis Frederick Valiton, Frank DesChamps, Abraham Bergh, Sarah Sadler, Wilbur Fisk Stone, Perley J. Wasson, Lewis Martin Link, Truman Curtis Link, Archibald Douglas Tolley, Delia K. Craddock, Charles Johnson, Robert J. Johnson, Willia Hamilton Johnson, Kenneth Chalmers.
"Antero Reservoir to be emptied this summer." www.denverwater.org/aboutus/pressroom/97788520-C34C-7AA4-A7F8C88879BDA3E3/.

Arapahoe County Hospital, Denver. http://www.worldcat.org/title/arapahoe
countyhospitaldenver/oclc/47813996.

"A Brief History of Stagecoaches."
http://genealogytrails.com/main/stagecoaches.html.

"Camp Funston." https://www.kshs.org/kansapedia/camp-funston/16692.

"The Chinese Experience in 19th Century America."
http://teachingresources.atlas.illinois.edu/chinese_exp/introduction04.html.

John M. Chivington.
https://www.pbs.org/weta/thewest/people/a_c/chivington.htm.

"Colorado Cave Yields Million-Year-Old Record . . ."
www.berkeley.edu/news/media/releases/2003/10/21_packrat.shtml.

"Colorado Cave Yields Trove of Ice Age Mammal Fossils."
http://news.nationalgeographic.com/news/pf/47378540.html.

Colorado Constitution, Article 22, Intoxicating Liquors
http://law.justia.com/constitution/colorado/cnart22.html

"Colorado, Denver and Phones." www.telcomhistory.org/vm/LHLocal
Phones.shtml.

"Colorado State Land Board withdraws South Park Leases in 4-1 vote."
http://westernvaluesproject.org/colorado-state-land-board-withdraws-south-
park-leases-in-4-1-vote/.

Colorado Statewide Prohibition, Measure 2 (1914).
ballotpedia.org/Colorado_Statewide_Prohibition,_Measure_2_(1914).

Colorado Wildlife Federation, South Park Updates.
http://coloradowildlife.org/news/south-park-updates.html.

"Congress Creates Colorado Territory." www.history.com/this-day-in-history
/congress-creates-colorado-territory.

www.DenverWater.org.

www.FindAGrave.com: Perley Wasson, Bradford H. DuBois, Cyrus G.
Richardson, Lewis Martin Link, Celsus Price Link, James Andrew Link,
Truman Curtis Link, Fred Henry Hammond, Archie Douglas Tolley,
Willia Hamilton Johnson, Kenneth W. Chalmers.

Henry P. Gillespie. Aspen Historical Society.
www.aspenhistorysociety.com/nugget_mining1.html.

"The Great Depression." www.history.com/topics/greatdepression/print.

"Halloween History." www.history.com/topics/halloween.

"Halloween Spending to Hit $8 Billion in 2012." business.time.com/2012/09/26/more-americans-planning-to-spend-money-on-halloween-and-pet-costumes-this-year/.

Hamlins Wizard Oil. www.hamlinswizardoil.com/index.php.

Harris, Pat and Fred. USGenWeb Archive Project, Buckskin Cemetery, Alma, Park County, Colorado. http://files.usgwarchives.net/co/park/cemeteries/buckskin.txt.

History Learning Site—Antibiotics. www.historylearningsite.co.uk/a-history-of-medicine/antibiotics/.

"The History of Antibiotics." www.healthychildren.org/English/health-issues/conditions/treatments/Pages/The-History-of-Antibiotics.aspx.

Holman Liver Pad Company. www.rdhinstl.com/mm/rs126.htm.

"A Hospital with History: Tewksbury Hospital, Public Health Museum, and Tewksbury State Cemetery." http://www.oddthingsiveseen.com/2014/04/a-hospital-with-history-tewksbury.html.

"How aspirin turned hero." www.opioids.com/heroin/heroinhistory.html.

"How Breckenridge resort got its name." www.blog.breckenridge.com.

"The Influenza Pandemic of 1918." virus.stanford.edu/uda/.

John F. Kennedy Presidential Library and Museum. www.jfklibrary.org/About-Us/News-and-Press/Press-Kit-November-22-1963.aspx.

Kohler, Judith. "Speak up for South Park, one of the region's last, great places." www.ourpubliclands.org/blog/speaksouthparkoneregion%E2%80%99slastgreatplaces.

"Made in America Christmas: Are You In?" http://abcnews.go.com/WN/mailform?id=14998335.

"Missouri in the Civil War." http://thomaslegion.net/americancivilwar/wikimissouricivilwar.html.

Montezuma County Sheriff's Office. www.montezumasheriff.org/SheriffHistory.

"Nervine: A Vintage Medication Pitched to Stressed Out Moms." http://blog.medfriendly.com/2012/05/nervine-vintage-medication-pitched-to.html.

"On Beyond Holcombe: H. G. G. Fink, Manufacturer." 1898revenues.blogspot.com/2011/07/on-beyond-holcombe-h-g-g-fink.html.

www.ParkCoArchives.org.

Population History of Denver 1880–1990.
http://physics.bu.edu/~redner/projects/population/cities/denver.html.

"Prior Appropriation Law."
http://water.state.co.us/surfacewater/swrights/pages/priorapprop.aspx.

"Repeal of Prohibition."
http://www2.potsdam.edu/hansondj/Controversies/1131
6637220.html#.UnHjmRDn_IU.

Saint Vrain Masonic Lodge #23. http://longmontmasons.com/colorado-history/centennial-1861-1961/doric-lodge-no-25-a-f-a-m/#more-262.

"The Stone Family History." http://judgestone.com/home.html.

"The Untold Story of Medicine." http://www.lydiapinkham.com/thestory.html.

"Use and Regulation of Marijuana." www.leg.state.co.us/lcs/ballothistory.nsf/.

"U.S. Entered World War I."
www.americaslibrary.gov/jb/jazz/jb_jazz_wwi_1.html.

"Vintage Medicine Ads of the Mid-1800s—Early 1900s." pharma.about.com
/od/Sales_and_Marketing/ss/Vintage-Medicine-Ads_6.htm.

"A Walk Through History: Traveling Tips for Colorado's Stagecoach
Passengers." http://archive.coloradoan.com/article/20121125/
COLUMNISTS162/311250051/A-Walk-Through-History-Traveling-tips-
Colorado-s-stagecoach-passengers.

"Warner's Safe Diabetes Cure."
warnerssafeblog.wordpress.com/2008/09/23/warners-safe-diabetes-cure/.

"What is it like to ride a Concord Stagecoach?"
http://www.historicthedalles.org/ stagecoach.htm.

World War I Selective Service System Draft Registration Cards, M1509.
http://www.archives.gov/research/military/ww1/draft-registration/.

About The Author

Former insurance underwriter Laura Van Dusen turned her back on the corporate world, left the Denver suburbs, and moved with her husband, Tom, to a cabin in the South Park area of central Colorado in 2010. Now the way home is through a maze of curving country roads, ending on a dead-end dirt path fifteen miles from a paved two-lane highway.

Her interest in history dates to age nine, when her parents bought a rambling 1890s Victorian home on fifteen acres near Larkspur, Colorado. As a child, she was fascinated by a collection of glass negatives found in the home's attic, showing likenesses of its first occupants. She would wander throughout the house and grounds, imagining tales about the people in the photos. She began writing that same year, when she received a diary as a Christmas gift.

Through the years, the Western history sections of bookstores and libraries became her haunts. Travelogues of family trips honed her writing skills, but it wasn't until the move to South Park that Laura started writing professionally.

Laura works part-time for the US Forest Service in the South Park Ranger District of Pike National Forest and seasonally for South Park City Museum. Both are in Fairplay, Colorado. She is a member of the board of directors of the South Park National Heritage Area and the Park County Local History Archives. Her articles have appeared in *Colorado Central Magazine*, the *Summit Daily*, the *Ute Country News*, and the *Park County Republican and Fairplay Flume*.